You're Uninvited

A collection of poetry and short fiction

Special Foreword Edition

WILL BROOKS

10 9 8 7 6 5 4 3 2 1

ISBN: 0692679782
ISBN-13: 978-0692679784 (Spargur, Brooks, and Associates)

DEDICATION

This book is dedicated to everyone, everywhere, for every reason. It is our experiences that give us our voice. May this collection give us all the power to speak and to share our happiness, our sadness, and every emotion in between.

A special dedication to the LGBT community whose voices are still struggling to be heard. Many of these works shed light on the hardships many in the LGBT community still face today. I hope these soon become a distant past.

CONTENTS

SHORT FICTION

ACKNOWLEDGMENTS

I would like to thank my beautiful partner, Lee, for always supporting me, and for putting up with me for all this time. I'd also like to thank my Introduction to Creative Writing class professor at Murray State University, Pamela Parker, who taught me the importance of imagery and rhythm in the written word. Lastly, I'd like to thank my family, friends, and mentors who made sure I never gave up. This is for all of you.

FOREWORD

This collection tells many different stories both happy and sad for different occasions and experiences including first love, crushes, self-acceptance, abuse, sexual assault, and suicide, but its main focus is the struggles and triumphs of LGBT youth, including my own.

As someone who writes mostly for my personal growth and emotional release, I never thought about the impact my writing would have on those who read it until my close friend Stephanie told me how my words had helped her through her own struggles, and insisted that other people needed to experience what I had written.

Writing, for me, has always been a very internal form of expression, a tool for getting out the entwined complexities that my mind couldn't arrange into coherent speech. With writing I can leave words out where I have none, or add words when I feel like I haven't said something enough. I can add commas everywhere when my mind takes a pause, and it's perfectly okay. I can use words I would never say in front of my grandmother, call it art, and no one will get offended.

To share my writing with you is both scary and exhilarating.

The experiences you are about to have, these stories, they are not easy. They come from a very dark place, a place of deep emotion, a black void, a place of seemingly no return that I hope none of you ever have to experience.

In order to shed light on what you are about to witness I need to share a little bit of my story.

I struggled with my sexuality from a very early age, almost as early as I can remember. I was different, that I knew, but at the time I had no inkling of just how different I was. I had all the cute little crushes and giggles that every kid has, but mine were for boys. At the time I didn't know that was "wrong" or "sinful" because I had never encountered anyone like me. I didn't even know what gay was. I was eight.

As I grew my attractions grew, and it was becoming more obvious that the guys around me were interested in things I wasn't. The girls got prettier and I took very little notice. Of course I had girlfriends because that was what boys did. They got girlfriends, but I knew something was missing. It just didn't feel "right."

I had my first revelatory experience the summer after my freshman year of high school. In that single moment everything made sense. I was gay and it felt amazing, not in the physical sense of being, but in the emotional sense of understanding. That light bulb lit up like it was the sun and shed light on all of the questions and feelings I had been trying to comprehend. It was exciting.

I wanted to share that excitement.

I don't remember exactly how, when, or what the circumstances were when I came out to my parents, but I know that it was right after summer camp and they yelled at me the entire way home. It was a rough 2 hours for a just-turned 15-year-old. That was the first time I had been confronted with the idea that who I was wasn't okay, that it was wrong.

What followed was complete hell. Three years of confrontation, of dealing with the typical "you'll get AIDS," or "it's just a phase" talks, of trying to become comfortable in my own skin. I had to redefine myself.

Being comfortable with yourself, and then being told that who you are is sinful and disgraceful leaves a mark you can't erase. It's like getting a scar, but the scar is your entire existence, and there's nothing you can do to hide it. You can't cover it with a jacket or makeup, you can't pass it off as a birthmark, and there's no good story to go with it, not like when you fell off the swing and cut your knee.

When you've been taken from the highest point of understanding in your life, to have that abrupt shift to the complete opposite side of the spectrum, when your personal epiphany is squandered by people who think they know what's best for you, that's when the darkness starts. It clouds your mind and your heart. It grows and festers despite your best efforts to light your own fire. Eventually it sucks the life out of you and throws you to the ground and stomps on your head until you've become the dust you lie on.

That's where I ended up. I can recall several times when I sat in my bedroom, tears streaming down my face with a pair of scissors places firmly against my wrists, searching for the courage to drag them down my arm and let the blood flow. I remember thinking about how much better it would be for me to jump in front of a truck, or to leap from my bedroom window three floors above the street.

But I didn't do it because my fear of dying was stronger than my fear of living.

I was one of the lucky ones. There are many who were not so fortunate.

The works in this book were composed and compiled over an eight-year period of hardships, victories,

14

and in-betweens. While the story continues for me, and for you, the story ended for many others.

In that eight-year time span, a crisis emerged that some of you may be aware of, but for many, it passed without much notice.

I'd like to take you back to Rutgers University in New Jersey. It's 2010, and an accomplished violin player and enthusiastic unicyclist enters his freshman year ready and excited to share his passion for music. His name is Tyler Clementi.

I'm sure some of you know of Tyler, but for those who don't here is his story. Tyler was a gay man, mostly closeted except for a few close friends and family members. He began coming out the summer after his high school graduation. For Tyler, his sexuality was still something of a difficult subject, but he was growing and learning to be himself.

Unfortunately, his sexuality became something of a topic of observation and study for his roommate, who set up a webcam to spy on him. His roommate caught him in a physically intimate act and broadcast it online for others to view. Tyler discovered this and saw that his roommate was going to make a second attempt.

Tyler also quickly learned that the invasion of privacy earned him a large amount of unwanted ridicule and scrutiny among his peers on social media. Unable to handle the pain and betrayal of trust, Tyler jumped from the George Washington Bridge and ended his life. He was only eighteen years old.

This is not the first time bullying has had such a profound effect on LGBT youth. Around this same time, numerous other teens and pre-teens chose to end their own life rather than continue to endure daily physical and emotional harm. The list is staggering: Jadin Bell (2013), Ryan Patrick Halligan (2003), Jamie Hubley (2015), Megan Meier (2006), Alyssa Moore (2015), Rehtaeh Parsons (2013), Audrie Pott (2012), Phoebe Prince (2010), Jamey Rodemeyer (2011), Amanda Todd (2012), Kenneth Weishuhn (2012). These are only a few of the many victims of bullying towards LGBT youth, but it is still too many.

I wrote many of my works to reflect the lost voices of these victims, named and unnamed. I wanted to do what I could to allow a silenced voice to be heard at a time when we all need to be listening. I tried to imagine their pain, their happiness, their fears, and their hopes and dreams. There is a laughter that we will never hear again, a voice that will never sound, a tear that will never fall, a smile that will never shine because someone somewhere thought these young souls weren't people, weren't human.

Someone decided it was okay to terrorize another person into thinking that the only way to be happy was to stop living, and that breaks my heart.

We have a responsibility to inspire people to be everything they were made to be, whether it be musicians, doctors, writers, lawyers, veterinarians, artists, or anything else they choose to be.

These are not my words. These are the untold stories of people who never got to share their happiness or their dreams. It is a collection of life, of hope, and hearts.

Be someone's voice in the world. Don't let the hate spread. We are all human, we are all dreamers, and we are all here to be happy. Don't you think everyone should get that chance? I do.

Be the reason someone breathes. Be the reason someone loves. Be the reason someone lives.

Best wishes to all,
Will Brooks

POEMS

Midnight

Green light forward,
red light back.
A lonely man walks
the fog-chilled streets,
no soul in sight.
The wind whips through
the narrow road.
A car speeds by
in the distance.
This is the street
someone before him
once walked now
deserted and dark.

Late Night Encounter

Fingers entwined
soft whispers in darkness
It's your face in the dim light;
Memories flood.

Soft skin I feel.
Can you hear it?
loud and heavy it beats;
two beat as one.

Cold is the air
but you are my blanket
and safety encompasses me;
safe from the world.

Silent lips are my muse
and you are my subject.
Still we lie and I
remember you; all of you.

But then I remember
words I once heard
"I can't make you love me
if you don't."

and I cry because
it's true, and I realize
it's time to move on;
move away.

But you draw me back
and you hold on,
holding me;
forgetting the world.

You smile and I see
the sun shining brightly.
You glow in the warmth,
I melt in affection.

I write in love,
in fear, in pain.
But I see your face,
I know it…

And it brings me
comfort.
You bring me
peace.

Love Poem No. 1

Shhh…
Listen…
Can you hear it?

      My heart beat.

it dances with the air
      it breathes with the trees
it pounds in the earth
      it burns with Passion's flame

Thump
      Thump
            Tha-thump
                  Tha-thump

Hear my finger whisper your name
Feel my eyes trace your skin

Your skin!
      Smooth
            like the breeze

Taste the music on your arms
Love the kisses from the clouds
Feel my arms around you
      hear my breath

Me.
You.

Love.

Dream Sequence

Whisper soft breezes to my imagination,
and tell the monkeys to swing from my ears.
Flowers sprout from my hair,
they adorn a bust of wood.
Tickle me with waterfalls and,
send the elephants to teach me silence.
Tigers prowl in the tall grass and,
I learn how to hunt.

Dried Tobacco

Do you know what a rope feels like in your hands?
Each fiber pulls and tears at the skin on your fingers,
carving the surface.

I remember each tug as I tie each knot.
Over, under, over, through, loop around,
pull tight.

Thirteen wraps make a hangman's noose, but
I only wrap ten 'cuz that's how many times
you said I should die.

Ten wraps won't kill me instantly.
That's fine by me 'cuz the Lord knows
I haven't suffered enough.

You laugh at me; you spit on me.
You push me down and call me names that
should run off only Satan's tongue.

But you speak them anyway.

Ten wraps of a rope and one knot on a barn rafter.

It's quiet in the rafters, no cows or horses,
only tobacco from this Fall's harvest,
hanging low, just like my rope.

Do you know what a rope feels like around your neck?

Can you imagine hanging, dangling, gasping
for a breath you know you can't inhale?

My feet kick because I can feel
the horror of my heart
beating faster and faster.

Ten times you said I should die.
Ten wraps of a noose.
Ten tears roll down my cheek.

Ten long minutes I swing from the rafters
as I feel my eyes close and my breathing stop.
And now all I am is your hatred swinging from a rope
among the dried tobacco.

Shadow

Fly, fly the bird
across the sea
into the night

Sing a tune of brightest day!
Oh, glorious day…

The Sun filtered through
rolling clouds
dim shadows on bare trees

Waiting, alone
silent

Snow of whitest white
a warm blanket
fresh footprints

Do you see it?
There!

Gone…

Love Poem No. 2

Kiss me!

No, not with urgency
      but with passion.

Slowly.
      live the moment
            slow-motion

Kiss me…
      Hold me…

Love me!

The Storm

I was wearing a red and green cast, the consequence of childhood stupidity. Outside, large chunks of snow were beginning to fall. Several inches were already on the ground, a young child's winter wonderland. I dropped onto my back and closed my eyes as the soft, white flakes landed on my face. I dragged my hands and feet side to side across the ground creating an angel of perfection. My guardian angel. I stood up and admired my work, the snow falling harder now, the wind whipping my face with razors of ice. I returned to the shelter of my house. I would have to wait to have my fun until after the storm was over.

June 28th, 1969

A voice, voiceless in a
puddle of mud.
A Stone Wall in the soil,
shelter in graveyard silence.
Mythical creatures fuel the fire,
and scared shadows shine
in cold sweat.
Blood-stained reputations,
secrets, revenge.
A stranger completes a prayer, his anthem
in exile, his madness under the moon.
The stars, unattainable by the hands
during a five-day storm,
fulfillment lost from a previous death.
Milk, a spoiled concoction
made for a crying baby,
and drunk with homemade cookies
that taste like copper.

Breakdown

Rain will fall today
clouds will dim the sky
no birds sing on tree tops

Lightning flashes
Thunder roars

drip drop
          rain dance
drip drop
          tears

grief stricken eyes
call on sympathetic whispers
and angels

two rings
          tossed aside
abandoned in boxes
          forgotten

He stands alone
at the table, adorned
White flowers and Candles

Forgotten words
          unspoken
Oaths of Life
          unfulfilled

no Hope left in hearts
or minds in pain
holes unmended

broken pieces
        shattered
empty wounds
        scarred

Love ended
Hate began

One heart became two
One beating in pain
the other, not at all…

Song Without Music

I'm tired of these games we play
where everything we do or say
is the first thing that comes to our minds.

Like shadows on the walls at night
that disappear with morning light
I can feel our two hearts slipping away.

This is not the life I wanted or the life I struggled for,
and now every time I close my eyes,
you're walking out the door.

I should've listened to your cries,
I should've answered to your pleas,
and now I'm right here crying, begging on my knees.

Don't leave me here alone,
don't rip my heart in two.
Forgive me, please, I'm sorry,
'cause I still love you.

Winter's Night

Traveling the cold of Winter's Night
hangs in the trees an eerie sight.
Long clammy fingers pull tight a thread.
A snap of fingers, a life now dead.

O, evil witch! O, Satan's Right Hand!
You keep forgotten secrets written in sand.
The blood of a bat, the eye of a newt;
what magic do you cast in such strange a suit?

A cold one rises, there, from the grave!
How slowly it follows, willing to obey.
It slithers and charms, seeking out a bite.
Too soon a scream in the cold Winter's Night.

This is How

Wash colors with cold water; wash whites with hot water; fold clothes as soon as they come out of the dryer, that way they won't wrinkle; remember to use a dryer sheet in each dryer load; this is how you fold a shirt; this is how you fold pants; this is how you fold towels; remember not to eat meals early; don't leave the oven on high; this is how you heat up soup; this is how you bake chicken; this is how you wash the dishes, and be sure to wash them as soon as you finish using them, or they will start to stink; remember to dry the dishes because you don't want mildew or water stains on them; this is how you mow the grass; this is how you put gas in the car; this is how you brush a wig; this is how you use a sewing pattern; this is how you iron pants, be sure to hang them so the crease remains nice; this is how you iron shirts, don't be afraid if you can't get all the wrinkles out; this is how you play baseball; this is how you throw a football; this is how you tell someone to go away, but tell them nicely, you don't want to hurt their feelings; this is how you get away from someone who won't stop talking; this is how you sweep the porch; remember to feed the cats, all of them, and make sure the kittens get some; don't let the cats in unless you know for sure Daddy isn't home; this is how you brush your teeth; this is how you wash your hair; this is how you pretend you took a shower, but be sure to wear deodorant if you do that; remember that "everyone can fly"; yes, you can fly, you just have to believe in yourself.

The Rose

Breath,
I inhaled the sweet smell
of roses that morning.
I reached down and
picked one, grasping
it lightly between
my fingers, tears
slowly crawling down my face.
I walked from the church,
the procession long. The hurt
made it longer.
Soon I placed that rose
on her mound of dirt
and stone.
If only this rose
knew how important it was
after the loss of a friend,
how important it was to her friends,
her family,
and to me.

Good Advice

Mom always said
> clean your room,
> pick up after yourself
> don't leave your dirty clothes lying around,
> take a shower everyday,
> brush your teeth,
> remember to smile.

My mom said many things to me over the years,
seventeen of which are nearly behind me.
Time flies, even when you're not having fun.

Mom always said
> live everyday as if it were your last, because you
> never know if you'll be waking up to see
> tomorrow's light.

And that's a scary thought.

She doesn't know it, but every now and then, my Mom
makes me think of death, and I don't want to die.

Letting Go

Come bearing no gifts
leave bearing no pain
ocean sand shifts and shifts
your love leaves deep stains
love me no reservations
leave me no broken hearts
sweet kisses of preservation
one life about to start
you are my minute and hour
my today and my tomorrow
my forever and my always
and I will never let you go

El Amor Que Murió

There once were two princes, kind brothers of sort,
who ruled distant lands from the Castle d'Mort.
Food was stable and peace was plenty,
and no man lived in a rickety shanty.
The princes shared all, every last thing,
but one prince grew jealous of a sacred ring.
Her name was Ariel, fairest in the land,
and the youngest prince did claim her hand.
It was love, the eldest prince knew,
but in hatred he did covet her too.
In his mind, brothers shared all,
and he wanted to share her most of all.
His fiery wrath fueled his plan,
he traveled far to vicious lands,
and met the King of Countries Feared,
here in blood a pact was seared.
He led his armies on a perilous march,
through two winters, the harshest of harsh,
and drove himself onto the Prince's lands,
killing all in sight with malicious hands.
While the King burned on through peaceful hillsides,
the eldest prince snuck in to hide
in the Prince's bedroom to behead,
his younger brother in his bed.
But he was gone, out fighting the battle,
the Prince was always quick to saddle
and ride to save his people dear,
and his bride who shed a tear.
There she was, like moonlight and silver,

laying on the bed in peaceful slumber.
"Ariel, Ariel," he whispered and sighed.
"When this is over, you will be mine."
She stirred and whispered, a sound like a dove.
"William, where are you? Is that you, my love?"
"He is slain, but do not despair.
I, his brother, am here to care
for you in his absence and loss of his life.
I'll love you the same if you'll be my wife."
She started to cry, but nodded her head
"If he's not returning, will you lay in my bed?"
And in that moment, he took her for his own,
while the Prince, still living, fought swords and stones.
The army advanced on Castle d'Mort's gates,
the Prince retreated and made a break
for the safety of walls and archers in towers.
The enemy was closing and would soon devour
the castle, the land, and all of the people,
the damage catastrophic and unbelievable.
The archers rained arrows down upon opposing forces,
soldiers charged out astride white horses.
Broad swords and heavy shields tensely braced
in desperate and very heated embrace.
The gate shattered down and there came a flood
of soldiers and weapons and both army's blood.
"Ariel!" the Prince cried, her life he must save.
He stared up the tower hoping to meet her gaze,
but when he looked up, she was not there,
the windows were closed, blocking his stare.
He feared her dead, already slain
in their bed, alone, where he this morning lay.
The Prince tried to make his way to the stairs,

but the enemy grabbed a hold of his hair,
and cut it, narrowly missing his head,
but the Prince spun around and killed him, dead.
The Prince was surrounded, the battle was lost,
but seeing Ariel was worth all the costs
of risking his life, to save all he could
and shedding his blood on metal and wood.
He fought sword and shield and pointed spear.
The clanging of metal was all he could hear.
Enemies lay around him sprawled on the ground,
and amidst all of this, he heard a single sound.
He heard his bride as she let out a laugh.
All was not lost! and he picked up a staff
and fought the hardest that he ever fought,
slaying enemies in dozens wearing iron-wrought
armor and helmets that couldn't withstand
the blow of the Prince's sword-wielding hand.
Victory was near, the end coming soon,
he would be with his bride before the rise of the moon.
But the next thing he knew was his enemy's blade,
and a final farewell to the Princess he bade,
for when he looked skyward to see his bride,
he saw his brother, his hands on her side,
and she looked at him with loving eyes.
The Prince let out one final cry,
and fell down to his knees in bitter despair,
the last thing he saw was her flowing hair.
He fell to the ground, eyes to the sun
no breath escaped him, not even one.
The Princess cried out when she saw her Prince
fall to the ground, his face no longer tense;
the life force that once flowed all through his veins

instead with expressions of love and of pain.
"You tricked me! You fool! You terrible beast!"
She said to the brother who'd just had his feast.
"You'll never have me. It's all in your head.
Don't you get it?" she asked, her words full of lead.
"Don't covet or take what someone else loves,
It's not yours to take, and it's not yours to hold.
Keep all that is yours and let all else be sin
throw all your cares and worries to the wind.
Happiness comes from the love in your heart,
not the ill will of mind, which stings like a dart.
You're better than that and your time will come,
and someone will finally catch you as the One.
Other's love isn't about you, it's about them
but if you can't see that, you will surely spend
the rest of your life just wondering how
you wasted all that time chasing down
they that never loved you the way you loved them
instead of searching for your own priceless gem."
And with those words she leapt from the edge
to sleep with her Prince on the cold stone hedge.

Her Body Remembers

Her body remembers
when she learned to ride a bike,
the wind whistling
through her hair.
Her body remembers
her first kiss,
his soft lips touching hers.
Her body remembers
the pain of losing a friend.
She cries when she
remembers the tangled
metal that use to be
a car.
Her body remembers
wearing her cap and gown,
holding the stiff paper
declaring her education.
Yes, her body remembers
all of these things,
but her heart remembers
the love of the one who told her
"I do, till death do us part."
Her heart remembers
her three young children
and those she holds most dear.

Almost Sonnet

We may not always see eye to eye,
but from the bottom of my heart, I promise I'll try.
I can't give you a heart of pure gold,
but I can offer you my coat when you're cold.
You're honest and different, things I'm not used to,
its not bad, I promise, they're two reasons I like you.
I can't always put my feelings into words,
but I know what I feel and I know who it's for.
I see in your eyes that you really care,
you make me feel the warmth in the air.
I don't know how to tell you all the ways I can see
or feel how you make my heart beat inside of me.
I know I can't be perfect, and that I do regret,
but let me try really hard and I think we'll be set.
I don't know how to say that I care a lot about you,
but I do, I really do, and I hope that you do too.

Ticonderoga

As I sit down to commence
constructing syllabic communication
on this thin white slate,
I think about the tool of the trade
resting silently on my desk
ready for work, like my Singapura
perched statuesque in the window,
staring at canaries and wishing
she could chase them.
No other tool is as beautiful.
The silver ruff adorning
its neck shows its superiority;
a Queen, an Alpha.
I pick it up, the smooth
glass finish feels sturdy,
yet fragile,
slick like I could exile it
with a quick flick of the wrist.
I can smell the dry
wooden scent as if my
mahogany desk materialized
in the center of towering cedars,
casting curious capers of light
that dance with the brisk breeze.
I remember the taste of it.
Masticating on a soft twig,
salivating at every gulp of
powder-dry wine.
Intoxicating.
I begin to etch my name.

Slowly. That sound takes me back,
dragging and scraping of graphite across page,
chalk on a sidewalk,
squares being drawn.
I think about my childhood,
and I grab my pencil,

and I write.

How Many More?

Sidewalks strewn across a city like toys
a lonely boy walks home
holding his head towards his shoes
'cuz he can't bear to watch the people pass by

The wind blows across the street
like a hammer it pounds the bench
at the bus stop covered in graffiti
and a message warning against outsiders

The boy cries silently watching
as each tear falls and
splashes on his jeans soaking into the fabric
spreading with each new drop

The bus comes and goes
but the boy doesn't get on
it's starting to get dark and the wind
blisters with the evening chill

He walks across the street
leaving his backpack to wait on the bench
and he climbs the tallest tree in the park
too high to see the ground

The boy knows every branch every knot
every crook This is his tree
There's a swinging rope
dangling from the strongest branch

The boy remembers the freedom
the power of swinging from that rope
he remembers the wind through his hair
and the sting of rope burn on his hands

That rope was happiness an escape
from the words and names and bullies
from the kids who didn't understand
form the kids who only knew how to hate

The boy took hold of that rope one more time
and he jumped once more feeling that wind
and the rope burn the freedom
but tonight…

That rope became the last escape
for a heart too broken
for a body too battered
and for a boy too hated to see another day

He was 13 with a full life ahead of him
he had so much energy and so much love to give
but all anyone cared about
was whether or not he liked boys

They called him names and threw punches
they chased him home and beat him with bats
they spit in his face and broke his nose
they hated him because he was different

Finally he had enough
he'd had so much he thought the only way out was to hang
himself in the park
in the middle of the night

How many more kids have to die
how may more have to suffer
how many more time do you have
to see these kids' pain before you ask

How
Many
More
?

Whore

I think now I understand
I was putty in your hands
But now I see that you're the slut
'cuz all you want to do is fuck.

Sorry I don't play your game
I always like to know their name
I'm glad that we're apart
'cuz now you can't mess with my heart.

Angel

Sing! My Angel
and let your voice soar!
You hold a voice
that comes from where
I know not.
Blinding beams of
harmonious light carried
you from the Heavens
into my arms.
If perfection had an
image, be it you!
Only something as pure as
diamonds could shine the
way your smile
brightens my day!
Gaze into my soul with
your deep green eyes
and let my knees weaken
before you!
I surrender all I am
so that I may have
all of you.
Perfect, sensible, unimaginable
You!
A day has not shined
brighter upon my face
but I give it all to you.
All that I am, all that I do,
Al that I can be,
let it be for you!

Vow

Take my life
don't let me be
I give all I am
for you and me.
You give me love
You give me life
I give you me
until I die.
Give me nothing
and keep me poor
because from you
I need nothing more.
From this day forward
I proudly stand
beside you forever
my hand in your hand.
I give you everything though
there's not much to give
but I give you my all
so that we both shall live.
I love you forever and
I promise that's true.
I'll never be unhappy
as long as you love me too!

Some Wounds Don't Heal

Wednesday. 10:00 AM.
I'm curled up on the couch
watching Rambo lick his paws,
purring loudly against the
living room's annoying silence.
Cats have it so easy.
They sleep all day, eat, poop,
play with invisible dust bunnies,
and then sleep some more.
When they want love, they get it,
or they can be alone.
Either way they're happy.
Not like me.
This couch is the only place
where the world spins a little slower,
the screams are a little quieter,
and the days seem a little brighter.
Mom's chocolate chip cookies
are baking, the warm scent filling
my lungs, helping me forget the
words I wish I'd never heard.
Where knives cut deep, words
cut deeper, dragging a trench
to my heart, through my heart.
"Don't listen to them," you tell me,
but I can't help it.
Their voices are the only ones
I hear. Every day. Every minute.

They poke and prod, tear and burn.
They replay through my mind
like a bad rap beat.
Worthless, ugly, stupid, disgusting.
When does it stop?
It doesn't.
I have my hood pulled up
over my eyes, but it doesn't
remove the sword buried
deep in my chest, or the
darkness swallowing me with each breath.
Mom is calling me from the kitchen,
asking where the scissors are.
She doesn't know they are already
cutting me open, because I'd
rather be alive like Rambo,
than dead like I am now.
I hear her footsteps in the hallway.
Blood is already staining the couch
when she comes around the corner.
She screams.
I look at her, tears falling
down my pale cheeks.
It's too late.
She knows.
She's talking to me, but I don't hear her.
The room is dissolving away to black,
my mom nods with understanding,
and for the first time in years,
I smile.

I Am Here

Cry.
Cry, my child
and rest your weary head.
Whisper silently
your heartache to me.
I am here.
You, my child, are safe.
Why are you troubled?
Breathe.
Breathe out your pain
and fill your lungs with life!
I am here.
I will hold you
in my arms.
I will protect you.
I am here.
and with me
you will be

Free!

I am here.

For Those of Us

For those of us who
scavenge for the scraps,
that little bit of food to fill our stomachs.
For those of us who
wander around alone, unnoticed,
unloved by friends or family.
Do not despair, for there are many
others like us.
Understand this. Life is a game
and all of us are merely players in it.
We must do what we can to survive,
to preserve ourselves.
For those of us who are alone,
no brothers or sisters, mothers or fathers,
aunts or uncles or cousins.
For those of us who
have no special bonds between us
and others, who we can call friends.
For those of us who are sick
and dying, day by day, hour by hour,
minute by minute, in this game of Life.
Remember to make the most of every day,
because we don't know if we'll see tomorrow,
and no one lives forever.

Poker

Hearts bubble with anticipation
as the Aces, burdened with
Diamonds, organize their
armies in an attempt to
overpower the Kings and Queens,
armed with sharp Spades
and heavy Clubs.

Short Utterances

I.
Bright shadows are all I see
and rolling cubes
every dimension every color has no
relation to the next
distortion

II.
Voiceless words uttered from
beneath a pool of
shining silver

III.
Somewhere in the dark
expanse of white a shatter
broke the heavy silence of
the awakening dawn

I Am Alive!

My mind is idle;
an empty cave perched strongly,
waiting for the wind to whistle by.
Birds chirp excitedly as their
fluttering wings carry them across
a water-colored sunrise and
white-tailed deer prance happily
in a lush meadow decorated with
wildflowers and silent butterflies.
The smell of Spring flows through
the air and fills my body with
warmth and spirit.
I am alive!

Sleepy Thoughts

I.

I'm lying awake with nothing to do.
I sure wish I could be holding you.
The bed is hard, the sheets rough.
Who knew loving you could be this tough?
A thousand miles walked and no ground gained.
The feet that carry are overly strained.
The nights are long and the thoughts are deep.
Somehow with you I'm losing too much sleep.

II.

Music's playing, the fan is blowing.
Where the Hell is my mind going?
"Now I lay me down to sleep,
I pray the Lord my soul to keep.
If I should die before I wake…"
Is my soul really at stake?
These words I send out to the dark.
What if Heaven is really stark?
Do I pray to God in whom I trust?
Or do I utter words that will turn to dust?

III.

Sometimes I lay awake
Wondering what's at stake.
Life behind this door?
Living is such a chore.
I want to sleep, sleep so deep,
But I lay awake counting sheep.

Love Poem No. 3

It's early morning,
the skies aren't yet blue,
and in the quiet,
I think of you.
Inside my heart pounds
an unsteady beat,
and your lips of roses
are might sweet.

The sun peaks higher
over the mountains.
I feel the heat of
a brand new day.
I see you smiling
out on the porch swing.
You take my hand and
we start to sway.

If only I could tell you
how I've felt since I saw you.

My heart was pounding.
Trumpets were sounding.
All I could see were
your eyes of blue.
You took my heart and
you held it close, then
we started dancing,
'neath the full moon.

Summer Air

Watching and waiting, listening
for someone to appear,
hoping I'll see them coming
to speak in my ear.
Sometimes I cry,
reaching up to the sky,
and wonder who I am,
but all I can hear are
two hearts beating swiftly
in the warm summer breeze.

Clouds rolling by in silence
tell me not to be afraid.
Ray shining down from Heaven
to brighten your face.
Our two hearts beat,
grass tickles our feet,
and flowers fill your hair.
All I need now is music
blowing through the warm
and soft summer air.

Road Trip

Midnight is where
we trade paper sticks
for light
and blond butterflies
for lions.

The Meaning

It's as awkward as talking to your professor while using the bathroom.

It's as weird as eating uncooked ramen noodles.

It's as embarrassing as dancing naked and being discovered by your entire family.

It's as beautiful as a nuclear explosion.

It's as sad as Sandy Hook.

It's as angry as a spouse catching a partner during infidelity.

It's as rich as the man who has nothing.

It's as inspiring as all the world's greatest heroes.

Campfire

dance
dance an orange glow
sizzle and
hiss silently
violently clashing crushing
kicking
shrink in time
grow in dry embrace
warp the world
ash to
dust

Our Story

Dry water pats my tongue
dirty soap sweats into pores
strings bounce on air
sweet salt sands my shelter
you carry hand with foot
tongue with eyes
heart with tears
we kiss the sky
dance the stars
swim the light
see the wind
with you
nothing makes sense

Rest Stop, Route 10

What are you doing?
Nothing you need to know, sir.
It is my business.

Where are you going?
Nowhere you need to know, sir.
It is my business.

Can I come with you?
Not in a million years, sir.
This is my journey.

When will you get there?
Does it matter? I'm leaving
and I won't look back.

Bottled Up

I see you
staring.
Full of desire.
You desire me.
I know
you want more.
You opened me,
tasted my sweetness.
You drank.
You drank more.
Threw me away.
Had too much.
No.
Not enough.
Open me again.
Tip me over.
Drink.
Discard.
But you'll always come back.
Always want more.
You crave it.
Addiction.
But I'm safe.
Trust me.
I'm a Doctor.

Never

beg for money
own a tiger
start a business
donate to charity
be the President
join the Army
or the Navy
or the Marines
or the National Guard
vote in elections
believe in God
have a wife
follow my dreams
live to the fullest
kiss a stranger
bed a woman
own a Porsche
kill a person
learn to say no
operate heavy machinery
condone gun violence
cheat on my husband
live on Mars
avoid taxes
live forever

Ponder This

How do you find your way,
if you don't know you're lost?

How do you know who you are,
if you've never given it much thought?

If we are able to change our voice,
why do we use the one we're born with?

What could you accomplish,
if you still believed in the magic from your childhood?

Damsels

Soft rose petals fall
on green grass.
They fall downward
to rest
silently.

Falling

It's calm.
All I can feel is the wind whipping my face.
My hair bends back, snapping behind me,
whispering encouragement.

My feet are free, dangling outwards,
my shoes battling the cold velocity.
I see nothing, eyes closed, nothing but a black veil
shrouding my future.

It feels so good to fall.
The feeling of weightlessness,
nausea, fear.
Peace.

My mind has no thought, only sounds
as the air whistles a pitch-less tune.
I hold my arms out, embracing the sky,
the wind, the earth.

It feels so good to fall, to fly,
to drift.
It's all I think about,
then,

nothing...

Self-Portrait

Bloomfield, where the roads are small,
and dad's spaghetti with meatballs.
I still can't figure out how he makes it taste so good.
Bluebirds, chicken fingers,
Rachmaninoff, and books I love to read.
James Patterson, my 11 cats: Panda, Oreo,
Rascal, Kit, Kitty, Mamma, Ferocious, Shadow,
Callie, Blacky, and Dieago.
Mozart and cheese pizza on the weekends.
Song birds singing Beethoven, and rabbits
waltzing to show tunes.
Striped shirts, slow and fast,
one true love.
J.R.R. Tolkien, choirs of saxophones, clarinets,
flutes, oboes, and bassoons.
Dancing, cute little beagle puppies,
sleeping to the sound of marimbas,
and J.K. Rowling.
Debussy, laptops,
trees, and xylophones, the one I played in
marching band.
Purple paper, red glasses, and swinging.
The crowded streets of New York and Chicago,
to the scenery of Richmond,
to the dwellings on Riverside Drive,
to the stores on Taylorsville Road.
Chopin and flowers,
backpacks, and vibraphones.
Yellow and pianos, the Steinway grand on stage.

C. S. Lewis and the Wright Brothers,
my mom, and my Volkswagen.
CD players, and rainbows.
Pencils and Schumann.
I am these things.
These things are me.

Insomnia

Tick. Tock.
One. Two.
Tick. Tock.
Three. Four.
Seconds slip silently into air.
Hands loom overhead.
Time trickles.
Triumphant.
Minutes mimicking singing songs,
melodious joy of silent night.
Tick. Tock.
Five. Six.
Tick. Tock.
Tick.
Tock.

Break Up

I can't.
Okay?
This is too much.
This is too hard.
Stop.
What's wrong?
Everything is wrong.
You were supposed to be my best friend.
You failed.
You left.
I cried.
You came back,
but not as my friend.
So I can't.
I can't change.
I can't forgive.
I can't love you.

You never loved me.

Tall, Dark, Handsome

Hey.
Hi.
How are you?
Good. You?
Good.

And I never saw you again.

Anti-Nursery Rhyme

When cold winds blow
and shadows grow
and night is all that's left,
the Thief arrives
with cloudy skies
and leaves the home bereft,
of happiness
and strong incense
and carefree happy times,
with hugs around
and gifts abound
but now they sit and cry.

Happy Place

The green shag carpet folds against my body.
It scratches, tears, burns.
My body lies still against it,
hands brushing the fibers,
breaths misting it in deep gulps.
I listen to it rustle against my ears.
This is home.
I sink low into its shallow depth,
It is where I belong.
Everything towers over me,
glaring, laughing, taunting.
I imagine flattening out against the carpet,
hoping it will swallow me.
I want to be the carpet,
to lay beneath it.
At least then your feet won't hurt me
when you stomp.

Weekend

Down, down in the depths you go,
Bitter tea of sweet release.
Warm my veins with flowing fire,
Turn my head with calming tease.
Drain my mind to blinding dark,
Dissolve my pain with freezing heat.
Lay me down on harder ground,
A sweeter bliss I'll never meet.

A Heart for Hope

What does your heart beat for?

My heart beats for me,
for health, dreams, life,
for happiness, excitement.
My heart beats for me.

What does your heart beat for?

My heart beats for family,
for comfort, peace, life,
for wealth, smiles.
My heart beats for family.

All good things.

And what does your heart beat for?

My heart beats for hope,
hope for tomorrow,
hope for people,
because this world has no hope.
Greed lines pockets.
Death fills streets.
Brothers fight.
Sisters scream.
We are full,
but we are empty.

My heart beats for hope,
because hope is all I have left.
I am weak.
I am poor.
I am hungry.

But I have hope.

Yes, my heart beats for hope,
because when you have nothing left to live for,
hope will keep you alive.

But Where is My God?

Your God blessed you,
Fed you in hunger,
Kept you in His arms.
But where is my God?

Your God clothed you,
Healed you in pain,
Wrapped you with his love.
But where is my God?

Your God sent you to war,
Smiled at your courage,
Praised you in victory.
But where is my God?

Your God guided you,
Supported you in hate,
Watched you send me away.
But where is my God?

Your God did everything for you,
Fought your battles,
Fueled your hate.

He called for laws
And fires, and stones.

He sent the darkness,

And grief, and fear.

And now here I am.
Alone.
Shaken.
Broken.
Dying.

Your God saved you.

But where is my God?

Pain Cuts Deep

Tears flow, burning
across my cheeks.
Your picture, torn,
scattered on the floor.
You were my father once.
You kicked me, stomped me,
punched me,
told me you'd beat the
man into me.
I feel the bruises
on my back.
Your belt still stings
my neck.
I can't rub it away.

This blade, beautiful,
shining in the dim lamp light
of the attic.
It's cold on my wrist.
I'm ready.
I can't breathe.
I push harder.
Drag.
Red flows, warm.
I'm cold.

I cry,
because I'm no longer in pain.

The air is crisp,
fresh, cool.
Still.
I feel free.
In life I'll always
be your son,
But in death
I can be the girl
I've always been.

For Lee

Toll the bells from highest heights,
rain the seed of glorious day.
Sing the keys of hallowed halls,
whisk the one in white away.
Flowered aisle of solemn vow,
endless token of pure love.
Gathered lights of now and past,
brightened smile like purest dove.
Take my hand and hold on tight,
for with you I'm never poor.
You are mine and I am yours,
partners now for evermore.

Merry-Go-Round

We kissed in my bedroom
for the first time, and my
heart jumped around like
a child in a bounce house.
You said you loved me.
The best I could do was smile,
but you were okay with that.
You could wait for me.
A week later you told me I
was a disgusting excuse for a
human and I should spend
my life alone.
You watched me cry
until I left for home
with a red face and lingering tears.
I vowed never to talk
to you again, to never cry
because of you, but we
ran into each other a few
days later and you apologized
with the sweetest voice I've
ever heard.
A moment later we were
kissing and I forgot why
I hated you.
I melted into your arms
like it was the last safe
place on the face of the Earth.
But you pushed me away again

at your friend's house party,
said I was too clingy,
that you needed your space.
I looked into your drunken eyes,
distant, cold. Serious.
I left and you didn't chase me.
I know you'll call me in a week
begging me to come back to you,
but I'm done riding this merry-go-round.

As Long as You Are Here

If I asked you to stay,
would you put me back together?
Could you find the missing pieces
that I lost along the way?
If tomorrow never comes,
could you hold me 'til forever?
Will you keep me in your arms
until the sun's last shining rays?

Can you feel my beating heart,
against the hand you placed upon me?
Do you wonder how the world could
ever make it beat at all?
If you could have one last request,
would you choose to stay forever?
Could you find a way to mend
the broken pieces of our souls?

I've seen the way you smile,
when you know that I am near,
so don't tell me you don't love me.
You have nothing to fear.

I don't need another night
to know we can make things right.
'cuz I know that you still love me
every time I'm in your sight.

Hold me tighter as the wind blows.
Keep me close as it gets dark.
I am yours and yours forever,
though I know sometimes it's hard
So keep your eyes on the horizon,
and let my heartbeat calm your fears.
Forever comes
as long as you are here.

Time for Change

When people count change for something to eat
Where a blind eye is turned to starving on streets
When earning a paycheck means being cheap
Where a trashcan salad is a delicacy
When the world is controlled by power and greed
And the death count climbs due to war and disease
Where love is not love for LGBT
And people with money break laws but go free
Where women are treated as lesser than he
And blamed for wearing short skirts and sleeves
That cause the rapes they try to flee
When the oil we drill starts killing the seas
And fish and lions and birds in the trees
When the ones you once loved can no longer see
Because you chose to spread hate with elaborate glee
Instead of showing love between you and thee
The death and destruction is easy to see
If you take a step back from your biased TV
Stop spreading the lies you constantly read
On your phones and in papers printed with speed
You are better than that please take it from me
Read this with heart and take cautious heed
The world needs our love and healthy green seeds
We can save the world and finally be free

SHORT FICTION

In and Out, Up and Down

I like guys. I've always liked guys. In elementary school my attention span was infinitely grasped as I watched them playing basketball, tackling in football, or swimming. I admired their torsos; defined, strong abs rippling with every movement. I sometimes daydreamed about how powerful those muscles would feel under my hands, all sweaty and shaking so violently my bones rattled. It was a fascinating curiosity, underdeveloped and misunderstood, but I couldn't ever get rid of it. It followed me everywhere I went; school was the worst. I would see the same guys, the cute ones, playing soccer during recess or basketball during PE. I couldn't lay a finger on why I found them so interesting, so enticing, but I liked the feeling; the feeling of being nervous and my adrenaline pumping. Somehow I knew these feelings were different and odd, but I didn't know why. The summer of 2006 is when I finally discovered what it all meant; when I experienced the most self-defining realization of my adolescent life. During the two weeks I spent at Kentucky's Summer Music Camp, that fascination and curiosity developed into my first crush; a crush on *the* perfect guy, Thomas Jones.

He was fourteen, same as I was, and he had the most

piercing blue eyes accenting his light golden brown hair. He stood level with me, eye to eye, mouth to mouth, and his skin was visibly soft and smooth; touching it was like holding a cloud in the palm of my hand. His chest was strong, like the ones I used to watch, firm beneath my hands while he held me close in his arms. Sometimes I thought about my mother, but frowned, knowing that she would never approve if she saw me holding hands or laying my head on Thomas; even knowing my behavior was against everything she had taught me, I still held onto Thomas everyday.

At night he would rest his head on my shoulder and I would run my fingers slowly through his thick hair, both of us breathing calmly and neither of us speaking a word. Other campers would pass by and I could hear their muddled whispers escaping from behind their cupped hands and see their scrunched faces and turned up noses. But eleven-o-clock would come and we would be removed to our separate rooms for the night, me being left with nothing but the sweet scent of his cologne on my shirt.

I cherished each of these nights, dreamed of them if I wore the same shirt doused with his scent; each one was memorable and special, but the most special night was the last night we spent together, the last night of camp.

The camp dance was well under way, campers jumping

crazily to the rock music pounding loudly over the amps, drowning out all of the opportunities to have a conversation. I stood against the wall across the room from the DJ as I watched Thomas dancing his heart out in the center of the room; center of attention. He winked at me, and jerked his head, inviting me over, but I smiled and shook my head no; I wasn't a dancer. He pouted his lips and batted his eyelashes, mouthing "please", but I stayed put. I watched him as he shrugged but went back to his dancing.

"Why don't you go out there?" my friend Kelsey asked. She leaned next to me and gestured towards Thomas.

"I'm not a dancer, I'll just embarrass myself," I replied. I turned to look at her.

"Do you think he cares? Look, it'd be cute, just go out there."

"I can't, I'll make a fool out of myself," I complained. I looked back out onto the dance floor to see Thomas headed my direction with his arms outstretched towards me.

"Come on, pleeeaaaseee!?" Thomas pleaded. He grabbed my arm and tried to pull me out onto the floor.

"No, I can't. I can't dance," I said. I tried to shake his hand off.

"I don't care, I just want to dance with you," he stated. Kelsey shot me the "I told you so" look. Thomas tugged at my arm again and I looked away, deciding what to do.

Thomas pulled again as the song changed to one much slower in pace. "If you won't jump up and down, at least slow dance with me."

I looked back at him, and then at the dance floor.

"Okay, that I can do," I said, grinning.

He pulled at my arm and led me semi-reluctantly to the center of the dance floor, spun me around, and pulled me close to him. I wrapped my arms around his back and laid my head on his shoulder; he did the same. I closed my eyes as we swayed in unison; I couldn't bear to see the expressions of the people around me, most likely looks of confusion and disgust. Thomas held me tightly and our feet stepped softly and carefully in time with the smooth rhythm of the music. I was in my own little paradise. Me, Thomas, and not a care in the world.

My breaths became heavier as I felt the adrenaline flow through my body, as my heart pulsed so powerfully, it might as well have been ripping a hole in my chest. The weight of Thomas's head left my shoulder and I looked up. He stopped dancing and took my face in his hands, his soft hands. I stared into his deep blue eyes staring back at me full of friendship and love.

"Don't ever forget me," he whispered, and he swiftly pulled my face to his. I felt his soft lips press against mine and suddenly the entire world dissolved around me leaving an endless background flowing with too many colors to name. I reached up behind his head and pulled his face closer to mine, never wanting it to stop; wanting to stretch that moment and make it last forever.

But that didn't happen. The song transitioned and the entire moment was ruined by a recap of loud, crazy party music that restarted the rambunctious mosh pit of campers. Thomas and I removed ourselves from the dance floor and rejoined our friends on the wall, all of whom had danced themselves out.

The dance ended with one last slow song and a slow trudge out of the basement, around the building, and into the lobby where campers crashed on couches, the floor, tables, or hitched an elevator ride to their floors. Thomas and I shared one last kiss before we both went to our separate rooms, and, eventually, our separate ways. Kentucky's Summer Music Camp was officially over.

Back at home, only 75 miles separated Thomas and I, but it felt likes thousands. We kept in contact by talking over the phone almost every single night, one thing my mom was always suspicious of. I knew she would never accept that I was talking to the same guy for almost an hour every night, so I tried not to hint to that fact. I always made sure that my mom was either two floors below me or outside a 100-foot radius of my position in the house. I was fourteen, too young to know anything about myself or to make any real decisions; at least that's what *she* said.

I, of course, thought differently. I was maturing and I was continuously learning more and more about myself, things that I knew were true that I knew she would never understand. I had heard all the hullabaloo about what she would say if she knew. "Oh, it's just a phase. You won't be like that forever. It'll pass," blah, blah, blah. I couldn't bear to have to go through those conversations, not yet anyway.

I had to keep quiet about my newfound sexuality, as much as I hated it; all the questions about who my girlfriend is, or why I don't have one. I couldn't break my mom's heart and tell her. I wanted to be able to tell her calmly in a civilized manner. I never dreamed she would find out the way she did.

Two months after the conclusion of Kentucky's Summer Music Camp I climbed into my bed, having just hung up the phone after talking to Thomas. As soon as my head hit the pillow, my door burst open and my lights snapped on, followed by my mother storming into my room.

"What the HELL was that?" she screamed. I jumped up out of my bed as she approached me, her hands firmly upon her hips, her hair pinned up in a tangled mess of a ponytail, and her face carrying a look of disgust and utter horror.

"What are you talking about?" I questioned back calmly. My heart pounded rapidly with adrenaline. *Oh God*, I thought. *What did I do now?*

"I just heard you tell another guy that you loved him!" she spat back.

"What? No I didn't," I lied. *How could she know that?*

"Yes you did, while you were on the phone," she blurted. I swallowed hard and stared back at her in shock.

"Were you eavesdropping on my phone call?!" I asked, losing my calmness, almost yelling at her. She just glared at me, not saying a word, but I knew the answer. I couldn't believe my mother would sink so low as to listening in on my phone calls. It just wasn't like her. "What's it to you, mom? So I said it to a guy. Big deal."

"Big deal? Big deal? This is not something you can brush off your shoulder," she retorted. She switched the weight of her body to her left foot and fiercely crossed her arms across her chest.

"What are you getting at, mom? What *is* the reason you're off your rocker?" I finally yelled at her. Right now, my mom was crazy. She was way out of line, and she hadn't even really told me why. I already knew why, but I wanted to hear her say it. I wanted her to tell me that she was upset, that she couldn't understand my choice, my lifestyle;

couldn't accept me.

She said nothing. She only glared at me, stared me down trying to compel me to give in. I stared back and rolled my tongue across the backs of my teeth and clenched my jaw so tightly I could feel the muscles stretch to their limits.

"What is it mom? What is the big deal? What is the whole reason you're in such a fit?" I asked being the smart-ass she knew all too well.

"Why? Just, why? That's all I can ask," she answered, her voice finally subsiding to one of civility. Her breathing had slowed significantly, but she was far from calm.

"Why what? I still don't know what you're asking," I lied. *Better not to tell her until she really wants to know,* I thought.

Mom uncrossed her arms and inhaled deeply, looking down and shifting her jaw back and forth from side to side, pondering about how to continue the interrogation. I stood in front of her, calming myself and trying to think of the best possible lie if it came down to that. *What can I tell her? What is believable and will keep me out of trouble?* I ran this question through my mind desperately searching for an answer. *I know, I could tell her-*

"Are you...g-...gay?"

And the question is finally asked. I was so relieved

to hear her finally ask it, but at the same time, so afraid. How was I supposed to answer that? Either answer of "yes" or "I think so" would spark the "It's just a phase" talk, which was inevitable in its coming. I didn't know what to say. I couldn't think of a lie fast enough, but I couldn't tell her the truth either. I just stood there gaping at her, opening and closing my mouth, too nervous to say anything without thinking of the consequences.

I finally let out a sigh and lifted my eyes in confession. "Yes, mom. I-I am."

She just stared back at me, no acceptance, no condemnation, nothing; she just stared. I stood there, shaking from head to toe, waiting for the talk of the century, but it never came. She bit her lip, turned on her heels, and left my room, closing the door quietly behind her, leaving me standing there dumbstruck with confusion and relief. I listened to the sound of her bedroom door closing with a "click" and then, silence.

I slowly crawled back into my bed and pulled the covers up around my neck just as a tear escaped my eye. Somehow, I was upset. I was crying because my mother knew the truth, because she said nothing to let me know her thoughts. I was crying because, somewhere deep down, I knew that I had disappointed my mother; knew I had made her sad, angry, and questioning herself; questioning her ability as a mother.

But she had always been a good mother. Not once had I even thought any differently. I remember when I broke my arm, every night she would sing me to sleep and tell me the cast would come off soon and that I could go back to playing outside and running around just like I used to. She always smiled and laughed at all of my jokes, even the ones that weren't funny. And she *always* made sure I brushed my teeth every morning and every night. But the night she found out I was gay, that smile disappeared, and she no longer laughed at things that weren't funny. Instead, she cried and prayed to God that I would see the light of day and be her little normal baby again.

That night was sleepless for her and for me. I laid awake and stared at the ceiling all night long, crying on occasions, trying to find some ounce of comfort in the pitch black surrounding me, but I knew there was none. I rolled out of bed in the morning tired, upset, and ready to jump in front of the next truck that rumbled by our house. It would've been less painful. I could tell my mother was thinking the same thing.

I saw her as she opened her bedroom door and stepped out into the light. She had deep purple bags under her eyes and her eyes were bloodshot red. She'd been crying all night, too. Neither of us said a word as I passed towards the bathroom; we diverted our eyes from each other and kept walking in our determined paths. I thought I'd be happy that she finally knew, that she could live no longer having to wonder, guess, or worry about me. I thought I would be relieved to know that I no longer had to live a lie, but the pain I felt in the pit of my stomach told me that I wasn't ready to tell, or live, the truth; but now I had to.

The following weeks were tense. Every time Mom would say my name my shoulders would raise and I would hold my breath, afraid of what she wanted to say. Usually she would just ask me to do something for her, and my shoulders would fall to a relaxed and relieved position, but sometimes she would want to talk about my "gayness" and I would throw her the "Don't even think about it" look, which would end the conversation without another word being said.

Those few weeks of hostility started the period of serious and severe depression. I stopped eating; sociability went out the window along with my respect for myself or for others. I was out of control. I carried knives to school and threatened my classmates; I threatened my stepdad, punched my brother and sister, yelled at everyone for the smallest comments and remarks, and threatened suicide. I was headed into a black abyss of which there was no return. I dug a hole so deep that the longest rope in the world wouldn't have been able to reach me.

I lost 20 pounds in two weeks from stress and lack of food. I forgot all about my friends, stopped going to church youth group; I stopped believing in God because I thought that he didn't care anymore and that he was out to smite me. I allowed Satan's demons to overpower me and take control. I wasn't myself at all. I hated everyone and everything, all because my mother couldn't stand me, or maybe because I just couldn't live with myself, gay and "out" to my mother, who was just confused. I didn't understand that she didn't hate me; I didn't know that she still loved me and was only having a hard time accepting me. I didn't know, because I never let her get a word out. I never let her say anything. I hated her because I could; because *I* didn't want to talk about it. Me, the one who wanted to tell the truth, who wanted my mother to understand, didn't want to talk about it; didn't want to try to describe what was going on in my head.

Mom couldn't take it any longer. I had to stop. I couldn't see what was happening to me or my family and friends; my life. Everything was turned upside down and I was too messed up to see it. Mom and Dad insisted that I get help, but I refused. I didn't want to talk about it, with her or with anyone. It was my business, mine, my own. No counselors, no therapists, no psychologists, nothing. No one could help me.

But Mom forced me to go anyway. She dragged me, reluctantly, to Dr. John Pemberton, a mental help/family crisis therapist. I didn't talk the entire ride there, and I would've blown up at my mother for taking me…if it hadn't helped me.

Dr. Pemberton helped clear up a lot of my issues and I was able to calm down, and talk with civility. Mom said she could see a difference right away; said the atmosphere in the room cleared from dull and gray to bright rays of light shining down from the warm sun; said I was visibly calmer. She was right, of course. I did feel better. All I needed was someone to talk to; someone to listen to me rant and let me solve my problems with myself in a calm manner. I just needed someone to talk to all along. If only I'd taken the chance with my mom when I needed it.

Life at home quickly returned to normal. I removed a lot of my hate and started talking to my friends and family again. I ate like I hadn't eaten in years, and I let my mom talk to me about my lifestyle, without getting upset. Of course it was awkward, but a conversation with my mom about my life always is. I'm always afraid of what she'll think. I love her, and I know she loves me, and that is what keeps me sane and happy. I know she'll never really understand everything or completely believe that I am the way I am; she's hopeful, but knowing I can talk to her about anything is a comfort, one that I know I will need today, tomorrow, and well into the future.

Scar

I have a scar. A huge scar, well, huge in my book. I've had it for many years now. Its red, veiny, and looks like something out of a science-fiction movie. People in high school would ask me if a caterpillar crawled under my skin and died.

"Yep!" *Of course not, dumb ass.* "It happened when I was five. The doctors couldn't get it out so they just left it there."

"Gross!"

"Nah. He's my little friend. I named him Peter."

If I make fun of it, no one else will do it for me. It was so easy to laugh away something so meaningless. It was nothing more than a mark from a playground accident when I was five.

But I have many scars and some are not so easily laughed away. These scars are hidden deep in the black sweeping seas of my heart, a place locked from the world like a prisoner in solitary confinement. Harsh words of ill-hearted adolescents can't reach it, or so I want to believe.

"Fag! Queer! Pecker-licker!" he would scream at me.

"What of it?" spoken more confidently than my

hanging head and drifting eyes.

"Where's your boyfriend?"

"Where's yours?"

"What did you say to me?" He squared me up.

"Where's. Yours?"

"Screw you!"

I never saw the punch coming. It landed squarely in my nose and sent me backwards into the lockers. The second punch I did see coming, but the best I could do was hold my hands up to shield my face. I counted ten more punches before he was pulled off of me. I never cried, I never said a word, I didn't even bleed, I just stood there backed up against the lockers willing to surrender.

I guess that was enough. No one hit me after that. No one called me names. No one tried to hurt me anymore. People said I didn't back down, that I was strong, that they couldn't hurt me.

That last part isn't true. They hurt me every day until then. The names they called me stuck with me. While the hole they created has healed, there is always a scar there to remind me of what happened, and how I can't let it happen again.

~~~

"And this is why you attempted suicide?" the therapist asked, writing something on his clipboard.

"Yes."

"Is this the only time?"

"No, that was just the first time."

Moonsprites

"If you aren't sure you've seen one, you certainly haven't. You would never forget the sight of a Moonsprite!"

"I saw one! I saw one!" Bobby yelled to a group of three of his friends one morning at school. He ran up to them just outside of their classroom.

"No way!"

"Impossible!"

"What?"

The group of friends couldn't believe their ears.

"It's true! I saw it last night!" Bobby said.

"Really? What did it look like?" Payton asked. Payton stood about a foot taller than the rest of the group. He stared Bobby down with a tensed face that read 'yeah right.'

"It was the most beautiful thing. It came down from the sky, right out of the stars. It was every color you can name, and every color you've never seen before. It came right through my window and danced in the moonlight just across the room," Bobby explained.

The other three kids listened, mouth agape as

Bobby continued.

"It made this amazing sound, like wind chimes across glittering diamonds."

"Wow!" Ella exclaimed.

"That's so cool!" Tommy echoed.

Questions started flying off their tongues wanting to know more about the impossible encounter being recited to them in the hallway. Ella wanted to know how long it was there, and Tommy asked if there was more than one.

Payton stood just behind the babbling interviewers, unmoved. At twelve years old, two years older than Bobby, Payton knew everything there was to know, which meant that Bobby certainly had not seen a Moonsprite.

Bobby was still answering questions, using his hands to describe the Moonsprite's movement around his room, and showing Ella and Tommy how big it was compared to his bed and window.

Payton watched skeptically until the explanation was nearly over.

"Okay, Bobby. I have one question. Moonsprites only appear when someone is really upset, and not just sad, but really hurt. What happened to make the Moonsprite appear?" Payton asked.

Bobby stared, out of words and out of story. The smile faded from his face.

"Something must have happened. Did you lose your teddy bear? Did your mommy yell at you?" Payton said, mockingly.

Bobby tried to say something, but the sounds caught in his throat.

"That's what I thought. You didn't see a Moonsprite. You're making it up," Payton said.

Ella and Tommy looked at Bobby who looked at the floor.

"I'm not making it up," Bobby mumbled.

"Then what happened?" Ella asked.

All three kids stared at Bobby, but he refused to answer.

"You lied," Payton said. "No one has ever seen a Moonsprite."

Bobby continued to hang his head. Ella, Tommy, and Payton turned and walked away leaving Bobby to stare at the dirty tile floor. He reached up and touched his chest, feeling the fresh, aching pain of the bruises that were starting to form.

"I did see a Moonsprite," Bobby said to the floor. One tear escaped across his cheek. "I see them every night."

Dear Journal

Dear Journal,

The passage of time is a bittersweet and fickle friend. It gives you more as it takes away. All that is ever wanted is more time do things we have to do, but then we lose the time to do the things that really shape who we are. More hours at work, less hours spending time with family and friends, more time to lounge, less time to exercise our bodies and minds, more time to be awake, less time to get the sleep we need. Time is constant, but it is also limited. You are time stamped. You are finite. You are expendable. You. Are. Already. Dead.

So in the time between nonexistence you have two choices: make something of yourself, or simply exist without purpose. A reason for living on Earth or not, you have a life and it is yours to live.

Do not hide for fear of death, but live because death is the ultimate end. Enrich lives, share knowledge, experience emotion, feel, touch, breathe, do, smell, talk, yell, laugh, cry, learn, love.

Whatever you do, make sure that you live.

~~~

Dear Journal,

   If words don't come easily, then they don't come at all. That's what music is for right? But what if the notes don't come easily, either? Music is supposed to be a language, a bridge between cultural barriers. But when the words can't be spoken and the notes can't be played, how then can I communicate? Music is my life, but all too often I find myself lost in my only true love. It's troubling to feel that the one thing that I thrive on and feel passion for, the only thing I know, even that lets me down. My life is filled with unfinished ideas, uninteresting facts, and disappointing memories. I am average. No, not average. Puny. I make no difference to myself.

~~~

Dear Journal,

   How can I feel ecstatic and depressed at the same time? It's as if I'm lost in my own emotional consciousness. Happiness creates anxiousness in the hopes that happiness will soon follow, but this is useless because the higher we climb in happiness, the further we will fall, and the pain will only hurt that much more. Isn't it better to be steady than to have the ups and downs? I find myself getting my hopes up

118

over things I have no control over, as if my desire for a good outcome alone will bring good fortune.

My heart is playing tug-of-war with my brain. My heart wants to do one thing but my experiences stored in my brain try to tell me what the best option is. Why can't I find the balance that is sly and elusive? Why can't I steady my heart and compromise with my brain? I have focused so much on the future that I've missed out on the things that are happening around me.

Now is the time to live! Now is when my life is happening! I'm not guaranteed tomorrow, but I spend so much time planning for it. What did I miss out on? What things could I have done better if I had only paid more attention to the people around me?

I'm supposed to enjoy college but I find myself just hoping the days will go by and that the stress will go away. I love what I do, but I feel so average. I meet the 'minimum requirements.' I'm not talented; I'm a hard worker. My brother is the talented one. Anything I can do, he can do ten times better, and that makes me the most jealous I've ever been. Why do I have to be the one who has to work at it? Why do I struggle to do things my peers can do? I don't hear chord progressions when I listen to music. I just hear music. This is my greatest flaw and in order to meet better standards, I will have to work twice as hard for twice as long. I will be an average teacher and an average performer because that's all I am. Average.

~~~

Dear Journal,

The air tonight is heavy. Sitting alone, it's so silent. I can hear everything. I can hear a lost watch ticking from across the room. I can hear my heart pound in my chest. I can hear plastic bags move even though there isn't a single molecule of moving air. Everything is still.

I find myself awake long after I should be asleep. I finished a book and I've set my morning alarm. The air conditioner just kicked on downstairs and immediately the sound of vibrating metal reverberates through the open vents. No cool air will reach my room though. It never does. Only the heat from the house as it rises.

I can hear my bones crack as I make the slightest movements, a sure sign that I'm getting older every minute. Age...years...death.

A powerful word, death. It carries such conviction. Death, the end of life, the end of feeling, then end of emotion. The end of being; existence. All life is...is a path to death. That's where all the crossroads lead to. That's where the journey ends. Everyone knows that one day they will die and cease to exist, cease to think, cease to teach, cease to learn.

Dogs bark outside. It's 3 in the morning and sleep still has not come to claim me. My bed is warm, but it does not welcome a weary head. It waits as my wandering mind splatters thoughtless words onto empty pages for no one to read except me.

And that damn dog won't shut up! It's menacing the way it barks at the dark as if accusing it of hiding the shadows of the evil in this world, but alas, evils walk both in the day and in the night. Maybe the dog senses the demons lurking outside and he feels obligated to warn whoever might be listening. I guess I could consider him an angel. If only I could comfort him in his time of panic.

Sleep begins to set in but I refuse to close my eyes. I want to listen to the night but my hand gets tired and soon I will drop the pen if I do not put it down willingly. I will sleep. Perhaps I will be blessed with dreams of what is to come, or at least happy dreams to relinquish my fears that whisper to me in the night.

Sweet dreams to those who sleep tonight. My prayers for those who don't. My prayers for those who are suffering and, my prayers for those whom I love.

~~~

Dear Journal,

There is never more conviction than there is in the thoughts of my teenage mind. What does conviction even mean? I write these five-dollar words onto paper as if I knew the meaning of every word I've ever written into this journal.

Something about today carries a heavy sense of wonder and uncertainty. I feel as if something just isn't right inside of me. My head is heavy and thoughts of death and pain are all that cross my heart. I wonder if that means I've gone into depression again. I remember what that felt like. Empty, cold, sad. I don't feel that today. I feel more peaceful than depressed. I'm very calm and some happy images begin to cross my mind, like those of hanging with friends, or my first kiss with someone I had been crushing on.

A thin smile begins to cross my face. The more I think about that first kiss, the brighter the day seems to become. I wonder if he feels the same way I do about the whole situation. I wonder if he thinks about me the same way I think about him. I know it's been five years, but even after all that time I still find my heart longing for his touch, his kisses.

Why does love pain me so? Is it too much to ask

that I love someone who will love me back? I want to love again, because to love is to feel, and not just feel, but to really love and know that love is keeping you alive.

It's funny, I talk about love as if I'm an expert, but I've only ever experienced it once. There have been other great guys out there, but I have never felt the same attraction or the same pull towards them. I'm not afraid to open up to anyone. I let nearly everyone into my heart because everyone needs a friend, or there may be a time when I'm the only friend someone has. I want to be there for someone when they really need it. Sometimes I just wish love was an easier emotion to experience.

~~~

Dear Journal,

I've never been one to hold a grudge or lie to save myself. I've never stolen anything and I've never pointed fingers. I was taught to treat others with respect in order to earn respect.

~~~

Dear Journal,

Right now I vow to never have my heart broken again.

It's not because I'm waiting for the right guy, it's because there won't be a guy, or a girl for that matter. Love is complicated, it is blind, it is time-consuming, it is mind-enveloping, it is heart-aching. Love is vicious, it is selfish, it is angry, it is remorseful, it is never satisfied. Love is hungry, it is empty, it is lustful, it is distracting, it is the end.

The only happiness is the pursuit of it. Happiness is not tangible, it is fleeting. Once you have it, it is gone. Once it's gone, you want more and you spend your whole life pursuing something you will never fully have. We spend all of our lives chasing dreams so that one day on our deathbed we can look back and say we did something with our lives. But that doesn't matter because when you die, you are alone. No one dies with you. No one holds your hand and goes with you to the Beyond. It is a journey you make alone. All of those people you live for won't go with you. You leave them behind.

Why spend your life dedicating it to someone who is only going to leave you when this life is over? Isn't it better to be alone knowing you have yourself, instead of putting your faith and trust in people who can and will disappoint you at any moment? I'm not going to make myself vulnerable anymore. I've locked up my heart and melted the key down, never to be used again. Only God and I know my heart, and I won't be sharing it anymore.

Dear Journal,

I'm out of line? Who's the one who dated Justin after promising me it would never happen? You. Who's the one who made sacrifices for the sake of your happiness? Me. Who's the one who has made every effort to keep you in my life? Me. You are the most unappreciative, ungrateful little bastard, and I want you out of my life. You never wanted to be in it anyway.

~~~

Dear Journal,

I don't know if I'll ever stop being angry with you. I've never experienced this amount of pain and the only person I can blame is you. You promised. You *promised*. You swore up and down that you wouldn't do this to me. How could you? How could you betray me like that? Are you happy with yourself? How can you live with that? I don't care how happy you are now. I don't care that you've finally opened up enough to let someone in. You will NEVER know how I feel. You will never be able to empathize. For someone who tries to put others first, you were a majorly selfish bitch. I can't believe I would ever try to trust you again. What else have you done to me that I don't know about? Do you lie to my face every time you open your mouth? Is there a reason you don't let me in? Is it because you are trying to hide your malicious ulterior motives? Are you really just a con-artist? Except, you steal heart and emotions, not money.

You took me for a fool and I fell right into your trap. I can't believe I could be so stupid. You played me like a gangster plays poker. He cheats, you don't play fair. I am just so pissed at you right now! I can't believe I could be so stupid! You have an inviting face and an empty heart. No, not empty, it doesn't even exist.

~~~

Dear Journal,

I promised myself I wouldn't take any more medicine. I promised myself that I would never get that bad again. I promised myself and God that I would never put people in difficult situations concerning me.

Yet, as I sit here I wonder if anything is worth it. I sit in class holding back tears that want to flow so eagerly. I begin to wonder if it would be better to cry.

No. I can't. I can't let anyone know that I want to crawl into bed, close my eyes, and never open them again.

They can't know that I secretly wish I could feel my heart stop pounding and lay idly by in my chest as I allow the blood to stop flowing and my brain to stop functioning.

It could be painless. I could take enough Vicodin to put me to sleep long before it relaxes my muscles to a point that they stop working altogether. I'd be nothing but a shell, a corpse that no one could bother ever again. I'd never have to see hate or hear insults that passerby throw at me without a thought of how it affects me.

They don't know that every word is a step closer to death, a deep permanent sleep.

I know in my mind that death isn't the answer, but in my heart, it's the only answer left. Sometimes I feel like I have nowhere else to turn. I don't want to go back to therapy. I don't want to talk about my problems. All I want to do is crawl away from the cruelty of the world, the hate, the fear, the abuse, the murder.

Ugh, will he ever stop talking? His voice is just so obnoxious. Just another thing I won't miss in death. Stupid teachers. Too stupid to see a kid ready to die, silently crying under their very noses. I wonder how much he'd care if I died.

I wonder how much anyone would care. Would anyone show up to my funeral? Would anyone even cry? My guess is no. I'm sure a few would shed some tears, but overall I'm just a wallflower that no one cares about. I'm single, have been for a while. I'm gay so the world automatically hates me, and I'm a college student so I'm broke as well.

Why am I still sitting here? Why haven't I just left and done it already? It's a five-minute walk to my room where no one would find me for several hours. It would be easy. I'd be able to die before someone could find me and get me to the hospital before my heart stopped beating. I'd be beyond saving. No resuscitation, no CPR, no help. Mom would be devastated, maybe, but she would learn to deal. She doesn't want a gay son anyway.

~~~~

Dear Journal,

How do you measure self-worth? I've plummeted to the bottom of whatever that scale may be. I have nothing. Everything is black. The world is gone. I am gone. I will never be again.

~~~

Dear Journal,

Sometimes suicide isn't about wanting to die.

Sometimes it's about taking control. When you've been fighting for so long, when your world has been revolving around everyone else; that moment when you take charge of your own life, when you decide what happens to you, that power, that strength, that freedom; it's euphoric, intoxicating. There's a thrill to knowing that you can choose to stop your own heart and push the selfish world aside, to stop the bickering and pain around you; to have peace.

I Remember You

I remember you, I thought as I saw your picture appear on my Facebook feed. It was your mom's post, not yours. We were never friends, but I remembered you instantly.

You were older now. The age showed in your unkempt beard and acne scars around your face and neck. Your blonde hair was down past your ears, greasy and clumped against your cheeks. I couldn't see your eyes in the picture, but I remembered they were blue, a gray-blue with deep, red veins surrounding them.

You were tall. You had always been tall. I can remember how you towered over me even when we were younger. Somehow you had managed to avoid putting on weight. I guess you were lucky that way.

A wide grin was on your face, so much so that you squinted as the corners of your mouth reached your ears. You were happy. You had every right to be. You were being set free.

No more orange or gray numbered jumpsuits for you, or gray walls and gray bars, or stale air, or sliding metal doors. It was your first day back. Your mom was standing next to you with tears streaming down her face and red puffy eyes that were nearly swollen shut. I imagined she had been crying all day, maybe even the day before, awaiting your release.

People were sharing comments of joy and hope, quoting verses, and thanking God for your safe return as if they had forgotten your sins.

But I remember.

I remember how it felt to scream. I remember how it felt to cry and no one hear me. I remember how it felt to beg you to stop, to leave me alone, to shutter at your touch, to bear it all in fear.

Do you remember?

How did it feel when you made my body wail out in pain? How did it feel when you saw my face covered in tears, my sobs only egging you on? How did it feel when you were inside me and my blood curdling scream rang out through the house? How did it feel when you shoved yourself down my throat until I vomited?

Did you enjoy it?

I remember quietly sobbing as you watched me clean up the blood. You smiled and inhaled the smell of fluids with a breath so deep I thought the world would go dark. My body shook, spasmed with weakness, with fear. I could taste my snot as it ran from my nose in waterfalls, but I couldn't wipe it away. You wouldn't let me.

Did it feel good to watch me clothe myself in something you hadn't ripped off of me? Did it feel good to watch me stumble down the stairs trying to mask the pain? Did it feel good to put your arm around me on the sofa and tell my parents I'd been a good boy?

I remember how much I hated you. I remember trying to tell my parents what you'd done. I remember crying because I couldn't find the words. I remember you telling me to keep it a secret. I remember keeping it a secret.

Why didn't it hurt you? How could you look into my pleading eyes and not stop? How could you find pleasure in terror? How could you be happy leaving prison knowing what you did?

I was five years old. You were thirteen. My parents trusted you. I trusted you, and you destroyed me. It seemed that everyone was so happy to see you home, so thrilled that you could be with your family and the friends you had to leave behind, but I cried when I saw your picture, because even after all these years, I remember you.

Passing Notes

Tucker,

      I missed you this weekend. Everything okay?

Sincerely,

Anna

Anna,

      I was sick. Couldn't leave the house. I'm good now.

Sincerely,

Tucker

Tucker,

      I'm glad you're okay. The movie was great. We can go some other time if you want.

Sincerely,

Anna

Anna,

      I would, but I'm really busy, 3 AP courses and stuff.

Sincerely,

Tucker

Tucker,

That's okay. Just let me know if you're ever free, I guess.

Sincerely,

Anna

~~~

Sarah,

Tucker bailed! I thought he liked me. Did you hear anything about it?

<3 Anna

Anna,

What? Did he say why?

<3 Sarah

Sarah,

He said he was sick. Couldn't leave the house. He said he's too busy to try again. Homework. What do I do?

<3 Anna

Anna,

      Sick? I saw him Saturday at the Ethan's. He looked fine. You need to ask him in person.

<3 Sarah

Sarah,

      You saw him at that party? Is he avoiding me? Did I do something wrong?

<3 Anna

Anna,

      I don't know what's going on. You'll have to ask him.

<3 Sarah

Sarah,

      Okay. I'll tell you what happens.

<3 Anna

~~~

Brandon,

      Anna wants to hang out. I told her I was sick this time. What do I do?

Tucker

Tucker,

Man, you gotta tell her the truth. She's going to find out.

Brandon

Brandon,

She's going to hate me. I promised.

Tucker

Tucker,

Bro, she will hear it from someone. There were a lot of people at that party. Someone saw and someone is going to tell.

Brandon

Brandon,

No way, man. If I tell her then everyone will know. I'm not ready for that.

Tucker

Tucker,

Everyone is going to find out one way or another. Either you tell her and she blabs, or someone else tells her, and she blabs, but she'll be angry. Your choice.

Brandon

Brandon,

Fuck. Fine. I'll tell her.

Tucker

~~~

Anna,

We need to talk.

Sincerely,

Tucker

Tucker,

Yes, we do. Sarah said she saw you this weekend. You weren't sick. What's going on?

Sincerely,

Anna

Anna,

I lied because... It doesn't matter. I will tell you later. Meet?

Sincerely,

Tucker

Tucker,

Aren't you too busy with AP homework?

Sincerely,

Anna

Anna,

Another lie. After school. Gym.

Sincerely,

Tucker

Tucker,

Fine.

Sincerely,

Anna

~~~

Sarah,

We talked yesterday. You aren't going to believe this!

<3 Anna

Anna,

Believe what?

<3 Sarah

Sarah,

Believe what Tucker told me! Ugh, I'm so pissed!

<3 Anna

Anna,

Why? What did he do?

<3 Sarah

~~~

Anna,

We need to meet. It's about Tucker.

Brandon

~~~

Sarah,

Just got a note from Brandon. He wants to meet. Something about Tucker.

<3 Anna

~~~

Brandon,

I'll meet you at lunch.

Anna

~ ~ ~

Sarah,

Help me! Please come to the girl's bathroom. I gave Ashley this note at lunch because I can't leave.

<3 Anna

~ ~ ~

Tucker,

I'm sorry. I'm so sorry I didn't get to tell you I was okay with everything. I wish you would've told me. I didn't want you to go. I didn't get to say goodbye. There are a lot of things I didn't get to say. I just want you to know that I didn't care that you were gay. I wish I would've said that sooner. You needed to hear it and I didn't think about how you were feeling when you told me. I'm so sorry.

<3 Anna

Tucker,

Come back. Please! Don't leave me here crying like this! You never told me anything was wrong. I would've helped you. I would have done anything for you. I can't stop crying as I write this. I miss you so much. I want to hear your voice. I want to see your face. I want one more kiss.

I can't remember the one you gave me at Ethan's party. I want to know what it felt like. Please come back! I can't stand not knowing. Please!

I love you so much! I always have, ever since we were in third grade. Don't leave me in this world alone! It hurts so bad.

I'll always remember you. I'll always miss you.

I love you,

Brandon

Revenge is Better Dealt

I approached him. Confusion rested on his face, anger enveloped mine. I stopped several feet from him, my back tense and my teeth clenched. He extended his arm, a sturdy bridge spanning treacherous waters, to shake the hand of a man he never knew he wronged. I took one grudging glance at it. One day there would be peace, but I stopped short of a return and stared coldly into his eyes, my breaths short and hot, flaring my nostrils. I could smell the humid dankness of rain not yet fallen hanging in the air. He stared back, warm and anxious, but I wanted him to be scared. Because he should be.

"Will..." He started, sorrow hung on his words. Maybe he *did* know he hurt me. "Will, I'm so sorry."

His eyes began to glisten with tears and the blood ran from his face. He opened his mouth to talk again but quickly shut it. I continued to glare at him. My breath steadied, my feet stayed planted firmly on the ground. I waited. Only silence momentarily broken by a distant rumble of thunder from the approaching storm. I held back my own tears. *No weakness,* I thought. He only stared back, but not at me, at the ground where his feet shuffled uncomfortably in the grass.

"Will, I know you must hate me right now. I can't say enough how sorry I am. I didn't know this would happen. It just did," he said, never looking up. I could hear his voice shake with every word.

"You didn't even tell me. You didn't even consider how I would feel," I said back. I stared at the mess of brown hair that stared back at me from the top of his head. "You just assumed this would be ok. You *assumed* I wouldn't have a problem with this."

"I didn't assume anything. I didn't think..."

"That's right, you didn't think. You didn't think at all. Not even once. Not about my feelings, or my situation, or my well-being. And the worst part? You told me right after my mother tried to kill herself."

He looked up and met my gaze for a short moment, long enough to know I hadn't looked away. I was still glaring at his pathetic attempt to apologize. He dropped his head again letting out a sigh.

"You don't understand, Will. This was his choice. He wanted this. He wanted to be happy. He wanted what you couldn't give him."

"What *I* couldn't give him? *I* gave him the world. *I* gave him everything I possibly *could*."

143

"You gave him nothing but pain."

"I gave him my heart! I gave him my life!"

"He came to me."

"You *took* him," I growled. He looked up, but only to my chest, fearful of meeting my gaze. Good.

"No, Will. You don..."

"YOU TOOK HIM FROM ME!"

"Will, I swear I didn't...."

My fists clenched. I could feel the heat in my head as the blood rushed to my face. I stepped forward and grabbed his jacket collar in both hands.

"You. Promised. YOU *PROMISED* NOTHING WOULD HAPPEN!" I shook him in my hands and gritted my teeth, nearly growling right in his face.

"Will, it wasn't me. I didn't know this would happen." His eyes shook with fear. They asked, no, they begged for mercy. *No weakness,* I reminded myself. He almost looked sincere, but beyond that beg for mercy, I saw his survival instincts kicking in. I saw his fear. I saw his lies. I saw his deceit.

"YOU LIAR!"

The first punch flew, taking him by surprise, landing with a crunch square on his jaw. He stumbled backwards a few feet and cupped his chin in his hand, his other arm out shielding himself from another blow.

"No, Will. Please. It's not what you think."

Lies.

I struck again, same place, and I heard a crack. He spun on his heels and fell to the ground. He let out a cry and tried to crawl away holding his jaw. I reached down and drug him back to his feet.

"P...pl...please forgive me," he stammered.

"So you admit it." It wasn't a question, and it fueled my rage.

"I'll never forgive you."

The third punch landed in his gut and he doubled over, crying out again before my knee met with his nose. He crashed to the ground again.

"Will... Please..."

"No!"

"P...p...please...."

"No! No, no no!"

I kicked at his back as hard as I could with each "no," recalling an old soccer kicking skill from high school. He tried to shield himself from the blows and I heard the crunching snap of his arm as it met with my foot.

"Will... P...p...please..." He was only able to whisper his plea.

"Please? Please? Haha. You're pathetic."

He was crying now. He cradled his broken arm and tears streamed down his face mixing with the metallic stench of blood that flowed from his broken nose.

He was weakened but my anger and adrenaline weren't. I stooped down and flipped him over, grabbed a hold of his jacket and lifted his face to mine. His jaw had begun to swell where I had broken it, and I could see a faint purple color showing through his skin. I stared into his eyes, no, into his soul... And I felt no pity.

"You betrayed me. And now I'm going to make you feel on the outside how I feel on the inside. You will know heartbreak, and loss, and pain. And you *will* suffer."

I pulled back my fist. One punch, two punches, three, four, five, six. He stopped screaming. I stopped counting, but I didn't stop punching. Tears filled my eyes and I just kept punching the blur of a man lying on the ground under me. A punch for the pain, a punch for the loss, a punch for the heartache, a punch for the anger, a punch for the betrayal. I couldn't stop crying, but I couldn't stop punching. He needed to pay. He needed to hurt. He needed to know exactly how I felt.

It felt like hours but it was only seconds, and when I finally stopped punching, when the tears quit flowing, when the anger turned to sadness and pain, when I finally stepped away, he wasn't recognizable anymore. I must have broken every bone in his face. His skin was no longer pale and smooth. Instead, in its place were bumps, cuts, bruises, blood. Lots of blood. Physical scars representing my emotional ones. Marks of my rage. Now he would always have a reminder of what he did to me.

I stared down at him, anger still giving way to pain. My ears rang with the sound of cracking bones. I could feel my hand throbbing and looked down to see three black and blue fingers and blood staining my knuckles. I had broken my own fingers in my rage and my pain. I clenched my fist and winced, and took one last glance at the man on the ground before me. He didn't make a sound, he didn't move. Only the rising and falling of his chest left me knowing the difference between serving 20 years in prison and a life sentence.

And that's where I left him. Beaten, unconscious, but alive. I left him an inch away from death, just like he left my heart an inch away from stopping. I left him begging for mercy, when he had given me none. I left him alive, but I was already dead.

I lumbered home feeling exhausted, clear, and incredibly satisfied, but I cried into my pillow that night because nothing I ever did was going to bring my husband back.

Nothing.

Forgotten

"Have we met? Do I know you?"

I was silent. I knew your name. Cameron. I never told you mine, you didn't need to know.

You studied my face. I guess the answers were there somewhere, but I knew exactly who you were.

We went to high school together. I used to watch you in the halls. Smooth skin, wavy brown hair. Perfection. I dreamt about you on occasions, crushed on you for years, but you were into girls, so I had no chance.

I guess you didn't remember the after-prom party. You were drunk and I was determined. I stole a kiss, one you returned later that night. You beat me up the day after, left me with a busted nose and a black eye.

I guess you just didn't remember. I knew you well, but when you asked, "Have we met? Do I know you?"

I answered back, "No. Never."

Petite Symphonie

The first time I picked up my saxophone in middle school was a moment of pure, uninhibited joy. It came in a black case with a red logo on it that said "Selmer," and it weighed a ton to my tiny eleven-year-old body. A plastic tag hung from the handle with my name, Leo Philips, printed neatly in the white space. When I opened the case it smelled like carpet does after you vacuum it, mixed with a sweet smell similar to my grandmother's perfume, but not as strong. The gold body glimmered in the bright fluorescent lights of the band room. When I picked it up slowly and carefully from the case, the imitation mother of pearl keys felt oily under my fingertips, but warm and smooth, too.

I didn't know how to play a single note, or what music was aside from the country songs I heard on the radio and the church hymns my mom would play at home on our piano, but I knew it was beautiful and I wanted to control the seemingly runaway force that could captivate an entire arena. The saxophone grasped tightly in my little fingers was my ticket into a completely unknown world.

Music would eventually become a passion and a constant pursuit—my current saxophone, a beautiful purple and gold piece of intricate metal, sits on a stand in my personal practice room—a life choice that would create impossible obstacles worthy of Hollywood blockbusters.

I remember my first professional gig in college. I was selected to play Reed 1 in a pit orchestra for a traveling Broadway show as it made a one-night stop in Paducah, a small Western Kentucky city on the banks of the Ohio River. It was a simple job, minimal rehearsal, quick and easy show, and a beautiful paycheck. Money wasn't the ultimate goal, but it helped pay the bills where working for a local, failing bakery and café did not.

Not a single person in the audience of that performance knew who I was, what I was playing, or a single thing about me—the orchestra personnel names were left out of the program—but I remember the applause that rang through the concert hall at the conclusion of the show and I couldn't stop smiling. My heart was pounding with love for music, for musicians, for actors and singers, and audience members who loved every second of it. That was my first real taste of life as a professional musician.

The next few years floated by in a back and forth state of working and not working, trying to make ends meet without giving up what I worked so hard to become. I moved away from Kentucky and pursued my dreams out west where the arts were blossoming as part of the tourist culture. Los Angeles had more opportunities than any eastern city I had ever visited. Gigs weren't easy to find, but I made friends with some local musicians and artists who had been networking for years, some of them decades, and I found my way onto the scene with their help. One person in particular helped me grow in every way imaginable and his name was Alan.

Alan was an L.A. native who had grown up in a family of painters. His mom had several of her works on display in coffee shops, casinos, and businesses, and his dad painted murals for schools and daycares, as well as performed live art shows on the sidewalks. Tourists loved his three-dimensional sidewalk art. Alan excelled at watercolors. The colors inspired him to paint his dreams and visions for a better world.

I had been admiring Alan for a while. His art was the talk of L.A., his shows brought troves of visitors, fellow artists, wealthy elites, and curious tourists. I had attended three of his gallery openings, the first one completely by accident—I was looking for a convenient store to fulfill my Twinkie craving—and I walked into the gallery by mistake. The next two were completely on purpose after I discovered a watercolor painting of a rose in a coffee shop and decided that I needed one of my own hanging in my apartment. I never got one, wealthier people kept outbidding me so I just enjoyed the experience of the show instead.

I met Alan in person at one of his art shows my friend Sara had dragged me to on a Saturday night. After unsuccessful bids for a piece of his work, and a bludgeoning headache, I really did not want to venture out of the apartment, but she insisted I meet some of the guests that she claimed to hold powerful positions in the entertainment industry. The art was beautiful, the entertainment industry contacts were exceptional, but the real display was Alan. He caught my attention from the moment I saw him leaning against a wall towards the back of the showroom with a glass of champagne in his left hand, and his phone in his right. From the vacant expression on his face I gathered that he was not enjoying the show as much as he thought he would.

That vacant expression, however, was almost completely lost in the perfectly messy mat of black hair that flowed across his head and down over his forehead. He had high cheekbones and large ears that folded outward, comically poking through the hair that tried to cover them. He was of average height, and he was thin without any bulk. The brown pair of penny loafers on his feet left a sliver of bare ankle visible where his black skinny jeans didn't quite meet the length of his legs. A blue shirt covered slightly by a gray vest with black buttons fell into every angle of his thin torso, meeting it curve for curve. Adorning his neck was a solid white bow tie that stood out against his outfit like a candle stands out in darkness.

He never looked up from his phone as I stared unashamedly at him from across the showroom. Whatever caused his apathy toward the buzz of patrons around him was enough to compel me to find a way to put a smile on his face. I found a way to politely ditch Sara who had been talking in my ear almost the entire night, and meandered my way through the growing crowd. When I was no more than just a few feet from him I tripped over my own clumsy feet and nearly crashed right into him. He caught me with bat-like reflexes, without spilling a drop of his champagne, and pushed me back upright.

"I'm so sorry," were the only words I could bring myself to utter as he stared at me.

He sighed. "It's fine. Kind of expected something awful to happen anyway," he said back with a distant expression.

I stared back at him. "What do you mean?"

"Well what else can you expect when you're in a room full of people who are all talking about your life which is on display, and they have no idea that you're even in the room?" he asked.

"What? You mean- Oh my god. You're Alan

Gutierrez!" My excitement dropped quickly as he continued to show complete dread in his eyes. "Sorry, I just, really enjoy your work. I've been to three of your shows already. I mean, I wasn't going to come to this one but my friend Sara said I should because she had people she wanted me to meet and then when I got here I saw it was your show and I was really excited because I just love what you do with your brush strokes and— I'm rambling aren't I?"

Alan cracked a small smile with the corner of his mouth. "Yes, you are, but it's okay. I appreciate it. At least you like it."

"You mean there are people here that don't?"

"I've heard a couple people say it was dreadful, but they were wearing all black with tons of eyeliner so they probably think everything is dreadful."

He stared at me and then burst out laughing. I laughed with him.

"I'm Leo, by the way."

"Alan. But you already knew that."

I smiled at him. "You know, most of the people here love your work. Maybe you should wander around more. I think I heard two guys fighting over who was going to buy the painting on the far wall. They might be having their own silent auction."

Alan leaned around me and looked at the far wall

where two well-dressed men were exchanging what appeared to be insults and a lot of exaggerated finger pointing.

"I should tell them it's not for sale and crush their dreams," Alan said. We both laughed again.

"I'd love to stay and talk more, but I'm sure my friend is looking for me, or drowning herself in champagne. It was very nice meeting you," I said and offered my hand. He shook it, gave me a nod, and I turned to leave.

I made three steps before I heard him call "Wait." He reached for my hand and placed a business card in it.

"I know it's overly formal, but I didn't have time to get a napkin. Um, would it be okay if we got coffee sometime? I mean, just as friends. Not a date. Just. Coffee. Unless you want it to be a date. Then. A date. Now I'm the one rambling."

I smiled and looked into his chocolate brown eyes. "I would love to go on a coffee date with you."

Alan appeared to melt at my response. The corners of his mouth reached his ears and I could see every single one of his bright white teeth. My heart nearly pounded out of my chest with excitement. I had a date with Alan Gutierrez.

I called him the next day and we agreed to meet at his favorite coffee shop called The Java Joint. I had never been there, but I had heard great things about their selection of authentic coffees, fresh sandwiches, and homemade vanilla ice cream. It seemed an appropriate place for a first date.

When I arrived and walked through the front door, I was impressed. The entire space was open and inviting. Colorful posters and paintings lined the walls, the rich aroma of freshly ground coffee beans wafted across the open floor, and the tables and chairs reminded me of a child's art room, not a coffee shop.

Alan was sitting about halfway between the back wall and the front door gently sipping from a steaming mug and reading from the Arts section of the newspaper. I walked up to him and sat down gently in the opposite chair—he didn't notice me—and waited for him to finish reading. When he went to turn the page, he jumped at the sight of me as my face appeared from behind the massive unfolded piece of print.

"Hello!" I said cheerfully.

"God, you scared me," he said with a smile. He placed his hand on his chest and caught his breath. "How long have you been there?"

"Only a minute or so. You looked really into what you were reading. I didn't want to bother you."

"It would've been okay. I was just reading about

some guy who was counterfeiting famous works and selling them on the Black Market. Apparently he was really good. It took them twenty years to catch him. I wish I could paint like that."

"If you painted like that, you'd be a nobody. Someone who only copies other people's work has no confidence in himself. You make something new and fresh that captivates people from all over. You should be proud of that."

Alan smiled and placed the folded paper in the chair next to him. "You really have a way with words. I like that. Can I get you a drink?"

"Oh, I can get my own coffee. Besides, you may decide you hate me in ten minutes," I said with a wink.

He laughed and said, "You might be right. Still, I want to. What do you want?"

"Caramel Frappuccino."

"You got it. Be right back."

He lifted himself out of his chair and walked up to the counter. I watched as his backside bounced back and forth in his tight jeans. A butt like that could stop people in their tracks. I hoped it looked that good bare and felt firm in my hands as he slowly kissed his way—

I had to hide the sudden stirring in my pants with a cross of my legs as he made his way back to the table carrying a milkshake glass filled to the brim with my Frappuccino and topped high with whipped cream.

He placed the drink in front of me and I thanked him as he returned to his seat.

"I hope you don't find this too forward, but I was wondering if you'd like to go to an event with me. I know we barely know each other, but I was told to bring a guest and I don't really have a lot of friends. It's a small showcase concert at Berkley and it's tonight," Alan said. He inhaled deeply and gave me an awkward panicked smile.

"You mean the New Music Recital?" I asked.

"Yeah, that one. My friend Amanda is in it."

"Amanda Pierce?"

"Yeah. You know her?"

"Not personally. She's friends with my friend Jake who's also in that. I was supposed to go with my friend Tiffany but she cancelled."

"So you'll go?" Alan asked excitedly.

"Definitely!" I replied.

The rest of the date flew by. Neither of us could stop talking. He talked about growing up and how he fell in love with watercolors. I talked about my love of music and the career path I was trying to follow. We laughed over jokes about Harry Potter and Star Wars, and shared embarrassing stories from our childhood. I never wanted to leave that spot. He had a warm aura when talking that captivated me in a way I had never experienced, like he was a radio announcer giving away tickets to a concert that happened ten years ago and the lucky winner would get to time travel to the past to watch it.

I wanted to take his hand and never let go. I could feel his energy reverberate across the table and into my chest. His lips moved with an urgent fluidity that made me want to reach across the table and press my face against his and tongue wrestle while fiddling with each other's—

"We should probably head over to Berkley. The recital starts at 7:30 and we don't want to be late," Alan said as I crossed my legs again.

"Oh yeah," I said, checking the time on my phone.

We stood to leave and as Alan quickly retrieved his bag from the chair beside him, the strap caught the corner of the table, lifting it and dumping the half-full coffee mugs onto the floor with a loud shatter. The entire coffee shop fell silent and all eyes turned towards us. Alan's cheeks flushed bright red as he struggled to maintain composure at the sight of the liquid mess. I bent down and started placing the glass shards in my hand and a barista brought over a stack of rags and began to sop up the spilled coffee. Alan stood behind us in embarrassment.

"Don't worry about it, Alan. It's just a spill. Come

on. I'll drive," I said to him as I handed the remains of the coffee mugs to the barista who thanked me with a half-smile. I nodded towards to door and Alan slowly put his feet in motion and followed me out onto the sidewalk where my car was parked. The sun triggered a sneeze out of both of us, which made us both laugh enough to put a smile on Alan's face.

The drive to Berkley was relaxing and full of chatter. Alan told me about a night when he thought he forgot to bring his art to a gallery opening and nearly panicked in fear, but when he arrived and tried to tell the operator that he would have to postpone for a couple of hours, the operator looked at him funny and said he had already brought everything and set it up the night before. Alan said the nervous jitters of relief that swept over him at that moment caused him to feint right into the operator's arms, and he had to be revived with a splash of cold water to the face.

I couldn't help but laugh at the tale. He was so cute, always worrying over nothing and succumbing to the embarrassment. I knew it wasn't a laughing matter—it was a very serious issue for Alan—but it only made him cuter, like a little puppy that kept tripping over its feet.

To try and make him feel better I told him about a gig I had where I loaded everything up as I usually did, but for some reason when I got to the venue I thought I had packed the wrong instruments. It turned out that I only needed my saxophone and not the three others I had packed into my trunk because I was at a one-night-only gig I had signed up for that was scheduled in between a regular gig and I got sidetracked somehow. It was embarrassing enough for me to feel a sudden increase in heart rate and a flash of heat across my skin.

Alan chuckled and said it did make him feel better, but he was jealous of my ability to handle it without feinting.

The rest of the night was smooth. The New Music Recital was interesting and beautiful as I expected—our friends performed like professionals—and the car ride back was peaceful. Alan fell asleep in the passenger seat with his elbow on the window and his hand pressed tightly to his cheek. I felt the calm of the evening pass through me like a cool breeze. The radio was set on a classical channel—I wasn't familiar with the piece that was playing—and the stars made a spectacular appearance on the horizon as L.A. drew closer.

I missed seeing the stars. Living in the heart of L.A., the night sky was always drowned out by the bright lights of the city nightlife. Seeing them now reminded me that the universe was vast and the big city I lived in was just a small part of everything there was to see.

When I dropped Alan off at his apartment, he thanked me for a great day and hoped we would get to do it again sometime. I agreed. He slowly pulled his tired body out of my car and walked up to his door, fiddled with the lock, and slipped quietly inside. I drove myself home and fell into a deep sleep as soon as my head hit the pillow.

The morning light came way too soon. I hit snooze on my alarm clock several times before I finally lifted myself from the pillow and rubbed my eyes. I stretched my arms and popped my neck as I stared passively at the blank wall of my bedroom. My phone buzzed on the side table. I reached for it and illuminated the screen. Three texts from Alan appeared and I smiled, but as I read them my happiness quickly turned to pain.

"Leo. I really enjoyed last night, but I can't see you again. I know I said I wanted to last night, but something has come up that I can't ignore. You are amazing and someone will be very lucky to have you. But it can't be me.

"I'm not who you think I am. I mean, I am everything I've told you, but there's more, and you shouldn't have to be a part of it.

"So I'm leaving L.A. I don't know

162

where I'm going, but I know it can't be
here. I'm sorry. This is the last time you
will hear from me. I'm so sorry. Hopefully
one day you can forgive me."

I felt my heart drop into my stomach. I had only
known him for a day, but I felt like I had known him for
much longer. He was perfect, sweet, caring, funny,
handsome, everything he needed to be. He was creative and
beyond talented, a real catch.

In the silence of my bedroom I began to cry. I
hated myself for crying over someone I barely knew, but I
felt as though I had lost someone I had known since birth.
The tears fell quickly with my crescendoing sobs. My
stomach churned with confusion. I fell back onto my bed
and pulled a pillow to my chest.

Everything disappeared; the sun, the bedroom, the
happiness, it was all gone. Alan was special, a real person
with real feelings and real dreams, and now he was gone
with nothing more than three text messages. Not even a
goodbye. Just three texts.

It hurt beyond what words could describe. There
was a hole, a gap inside me that continued to rip as I lay on
my bed and cried. I felt like I had lost something that was a
part of me. I wanted the world to go dark and let me sleep,

let me dream so I could believe it was all just a horrible nightmare. I wanted it not to be true. I kept looking at my phone hoping those messages were not displayed on my screen, that Alan was still waiting for me to call, waiting for me to laugh with him, and tell stories on long car rides. I just wanted him to be there.

But he was gone. He had been a genre of music I had never heard. He was his own symphony, written with each beautiful word that passed his lips. For a day he was the never-ending song playing in my head, but now, here in my bed with tears streaming down my face, I couldn't hear any music. The song stopped playing and behind it there was nothing. No sound. No melody of the sun, or the city, or the birds, or people on the sidewalk. The world was empty, and so was I.

It was stupid to feel the way I did, childish even, but under the comfort of my blanket I sobbed until the silence began to feel less foreign. As my breath calmed I found the strength to get out of bed and face the day.

The music slowly returned to my life, but the song I heard with Alan has never been repeated. The melodies are still sweet and the symphonies are powerful, but life had already given me its best work. Now everything is faded like an old photograph, beautiful but lacking something. Maybe one day I'll find that missing piece, but today I'm just thankful for what I have.

An Icy Passing

It's a cruel thing to do to oneself, lying out half-naked in the snow, feeling the tiny crystals numb your body and slowly watching them melt on your skin. You've been lying there so stiff, so used to the cold, that your body has forgotten how to shiver.

Your stomach slowly rises and falls, each new flake landing there becoming nothing but a clear droplet, rolling and pooling in your navel. You breathe through your mouth, watching each warm cloud float away and dissipate. A quick breeze blows swiftly across your body, chilling, stinging, yet you still don't move a finger.

Today is the perfect day. Everything is how it should be, ideal, the cold, the snow, the solitude. You've dreamed of this day, taken note of it, kept it alive in your imagination.

Staring into the darkened, swirling abyss above, you know the sun is up there and with it, is warmth. Snowflakes drift down flying, swirling, the intensity climbing, the air thickening as the bare, tangled trees sway, casting subtle shadows across your face. A thin blanket of snow drifts across your body, soft, cold, perfect, slowly liquefying and refreezing, a repeating cycle.

You close your eyes, the temperature taking over, and your heart begins to race, waking your stationary body to the reality surrounding it. Your breathing becomes heavy, and you can feel the blood speeding through your veins. It won't be long now, not long at all. Your eyes snap open and you can see the light, it's right there, inches from your outstretched fingertips, its heat filling you, calming you, calling you.

You can feel your body lifting, stretching towards the light, leaving the ground, the snow, the wind, the light's rays as bright as ever, almost blinding, yet so beautiful. You steal one glance to your side, and you see yourself still lying motionless in the snow, your eyes still open, yet the crystals no longer melt on your cold, hard skin.

Fourteen Lines

I found the poem you wrote me. You didn't pen the words; you copied Shakespeare's Eighteenth Sonnet onto a piece of notebook paper and sent it to me for Valentine's Day inside a Hallmark card you had signed with your chicken scratch of a signature. I remember the card because it had a Dalmatian on the front and it barked, "I ruff you." I wish I still had that card.

Although the words weren't yours originally, I understood the purpose and I cherished it with just as much love as I would have any other gift. The penciled letters have started to smear against the white background, especially in the folds where the creases rubbed together between the pages of the notebook it was tucked in. I can still make out most of the words, and when I read them silently to myself I can hear you reciting it to me like you did when I flew out to see you. You stared right into my eyes and let me know that you meant every single 16th century word.

Remembering that moment used to give me butterflies. You were so handsome, dressed in your blue suit and favorite tie, the one with silver stars on it, with your brown hair slicked back in dapper 1950's fashion. It was snowing outside and you took me to see the Quad at your university. I remember the pictures you had shown me from that Fall with the trees adorned in orange and red, and the grass still green as it was in Spring, but that night it was blanketed in a fresh white dusting. You said it was your favorite spot during Winter. I made it mine in that moment.

We held hands and watched as the snow continued to fall. I had never heard silence so beautiful until that night, and I've never heard it since. You smelled sweet, like the honeysuckle back home, and I breathed deeply, filling my lungs with your aroma. A snowflake fell on my nose and you gently brushed it away. I smiled as my eyes met your gaze, your chocolate brown eyes unblinking against the chilly breeze that cut its way through the shadowed buildings outlining the Quad.

I opened my mouth to speak, but you slowly raised a finger and pressed it against my lips. In that captive instant you spoke Shakespeare's sonnet with such conviction that I could have believed you were the Bard's reincarnation. Your voice was smooth despite the frozen air that dried our skin. The words entered my soul like a hymn, lifting me. The ground ceased to exist. We were truly floating. My heart pounded and suddenly the world faded to grey and the air sprung to life. For a moment you were the only thing in the world that mattered. You were there with me, professing your love the best way you knew how, and I fell. With your final words I fell into your arms, into your lips, into your breath.

Kissing you for the first time was like tasting alcohol for the first time before turning twenty-one; sweet, inviting, warm, and with a slight head rush from the excitement. I could feel my blood pulsing through my veins as my heart beat faster against the heat radiating between us. The wind was no longer cold, and it was energized against the setting sun and cascading white, heightening my awareness that you were falling, too.

When you finally pulled away, I could still taste the wintergreen gum you had been chewing. I smiled so hard I thought I might touch my ears with the corners of my mouth. You smiled back and even in the approaching darkness I could see you turn as red as the scarf I was wearing. I fell again into your arms and melted into your embrace.

That was the happiest Christmas I can remember. By the time your card arrived in the mail for Valentine's Day, the novelty had worn off. We never saw each other, we could barely keep in contact long enough to call what we had a relationship, but you sent me the sonnet reminding me that you cared, that you would always care.

We broke up years ago—I'm now married to a wonderful man—but for some reason I kept this small token of your affection. Maybe I was hoping the sonnet would remind me of all the good times we had, as if discarding the piece of paper would also discard the memories. Perhaps I thought that one day things would be different, that we would pick up where we left off, and we would fall again into each other like we did that night. Or it's possible that I just didn't know how to let go, didn't want to let go of someone who was able to steal my heart with fourteen lines of eloquent speech while snow fell silently around us.

Whatever the reason, when I found the scribbled sonnet tucked away in my notebook I remembered that night, and I felt no butterflies, no nervous shivers of longing. Instead, I smiled because I knew we had both found our happiness in other people, and I no longer needed to hold on to something that no longer existed.

With one last glance at the messy pencil markings I refolded the paper along its original creases and watched as it slipped from my fingers and slowly descended into the flames of the crackling fire blazing in my fireplace. I took a deep breath and exhaled a sigh of relief as the last remnants of the sonnet curled, blackened, and ultimately crumbled into the ashes.

"What was that?" my husband asked. I had not heard him enter the room. He shouldered our one-year-old

171

daughter who was fast asleep.

"Just an old note," I replied. "Nothing important."

I gave him a kiss, and lightly brushed our daughter's hair with my finger.

"I love you," he said.

"I love you, too."

The Most Important Thing

There's no other name for this place than perfection. It's the kind of place I like to refer to as Old Folk Heaven, a place where elderly women sit outside on their porch swings sipping sweet tea and gossiping about the single neighbor lady who has one too many handymen, and where the men guzzle longnecks in the gas station after a long day of farming. It's the kind of place where kids walk around town, where people leave their front doors unlocked all day, where everyone uses first names regardless of age.

It's the place I left when I went to college, a place I never thought I'd look back on when I married the man of my dreams, but six years of rude and selfish Chicago city dwellers left me yearning for something less frantic, for a place with towering shade trees and fresh air. And grass. I wanted a home with a yard, and flowers, and an actual mailbox I could stroll to in the morning with a mug of fresh coffee, smiling while the elderly neighbors walked their dog and laughed at cheesy jokes. I would greet them and then walk back inside, the smell of pancakes welcoming me into the kitchen where my family would be pleasantly chatting about anything and everything.

My husband, Derek, wasn't as excited about the idea of living in a small town as I was, constantly bringing up fears of prejudice and persecution from a community of people who didn't like having their way of life interrupted. I remember him saying that small towns were for people too civilized for the civilized world. I never understood what he meant by that. I think his greatest fear was that our four-year-old son, Michael, would be bullied for having two dads when he started Kindergarten. The thought had crossed my mind, but I was confident that we, as parents, could handle the situation if and when it arose. Finally, after a year of coaxing with the real estate ads, and a lot of reassurance, Derek and I closed the deal on a small, two story, three-bedroom home.

We moved in a week later and after finally feeling settled, everything seemed to go wrong. It felt as if the air surrounding our home had a muggy weight to it, like fog, but thicker, bringing agony and turmoil with it, testing our patience every few days. Derek and I had been dealing with a group of teenagers who were known by the locals for ripping up mailboxes and setting small fires. We were doing our best to passively fight the constant tirade of attacks on our home – the first being a simple green spray-paint job of the word *QUEERS* across our front door – and doing our best to keep Michael out of harm's way.

The paint barely had a chance to dry before Derek and I bolted upright in bed in the middle of the night to the sounds of laughter and crunching metal intruding through our open window. We threw open our front door just in time to see a rusty, old pick-up tearing down the street and two teenagers in red hoodies tossing our mailbox into our front yard, yanked straight out of the ground and flattened. One of them managed to yell out a few choice insults before disappearing around the curve at the end of the street. Derek let out a sigh, staring at the mangled metal as if it were an unwelcome guest. I wanted to hug him but he tensed up, so I squeezed his shoulder instead and directed us back inside.

Michael quietly entered the living room as we closed the door. He was startled, having heard the loud noises, and asked us if it was going to storm and if he could sleep with us. Derek and I could only look at each other before reassuring Michael that everything was okay and that he could sleep in his own bed.

"Maybe we should call the police," Derek said after hearing Michael's door click shut.

"No, I don't think it's worth the trouble right now," I said. "It's only a bunch of teenagers."

"I just don't want this getting out of hand."

"It won't. I promise."

"Alright," he sighed. I wrapped my arms around him, holding him like a mother holds a frightened child, and kissed him before crawling back into bed.

Derek bought and installed a new mailbox the next day and everything was fine for a couple of weeks. The Rebels – as we learned they were called – were only causing minor headaches by ripping up flowers or spray painting uncreative names on our door, which we continued to paint over. I frequently found Derek out in the garage tinkering with small appliances, his way of dealing with the vandalism. He never fixed anything, just took it apart and left it in pieces, hoping later to reassemble it as if it never came apart in the first place. I knew he wanted to say something, to call the police or to try to catch the Hooligans ourselves, but I kept insisting that it would blow over like a storm, or the Bush Administration - he always cracked a smile when I said that - and that we just needed to wait a little longer.

On the Sunday after Easter, Derek and I escorted Michael to a play date with a young boy named Bobby just down the road about a half-mile or so. Bobby's parents, Mike and Trish, were young and new to the small town just as we were. Michael and Bobby were instant friends, fighting demons with magic wands and building blanket forts to keep the parents out, something Derek did with him at home when I wanted to play 'bored' games. Derek and I had just finished telling the embellished story of how we met when three fire trucks sped past the house in a flash of red, sirens screaming an earsplitting call of warning. I looked out the window just long enough to see the rusty, old pick-up flying in the opposite direction, the Rebels screaming and cheering. My heart began racing and I excused myself for a moment to step onto the front porch. Immediately I could smell the rough, stinging tinge of wood burning as a rolling, black cloud of ash tainted the air. I peered down the street, watching as the fire trucks turned into a driveway. My driveway. My stomach turned to mush and my heart raced like it did on my wedding day. I ran back inside.

"Derek, we need to go," I said, half inside, half outside, holding the doorknob tightly in my hand.

"What's wrong?" Derek asked, standing quickly.

"We just...have to go," I said. I turned to Trish seated on the sofa. "Can you watch Michael for a bit? We have an emergency."

Without waiting for an answer, I grabbed Derek by

the hand and pulled him outside, scrambling to get my keys out of my pocket.

"What's wrong?" Derek asked, coughing in the smoke.

"Someone set fire to our house."

"What?!" He stared down the street. "Shit!"

Derek's body tensed and he starting running down the street towards our house. I jumped in the car and started it knowing I couldn't keep up with Derek on foot - he was already halfway down the street by the time I got the car out of the driveway - and accelerated to catch up. The black smoke swirled in the gusts of wind brought on by an approaching storm front, and I could barely make out the pavement blurring by. It was like searching for fish in a muddy river at night.

The driveway was covered in firemen and trucks, all battling the blaze that luckily only engulfed our garage. I parked the car and found Derek, statuesque, staring at the building flickering bright orange. He didn't speak. He didn't move. The searing heat licked my face and sweat beaded on Derek's forehead. He just stared. I reached for his hand but he jerked away, turning his back to me as he did.

"This is too much. I can't do this," and he walked off toward the creek in front of our house, squeezing the bridge of his nose right between his eyes. I wanted to follow but my feet glued themselves to the concrete.

I turned back to the burning garage, the heat died down as the firefighters controlled and eventually extinguished the blaze. Steam rose from the sizzling ashes, remnants of memories of things we wanted - and didn't want - to remember, once piled high in flimsy cardboard boxes. It was gone. All of it. Derek was sitting on the creek bed now, his head on his knees, shoulders slightly shaking like a frightened kitten. He was crying, something I'd only seen him do once before. I slowly approached him amongst the disintegrating chaos and joined him on the creek bed.

"I'm scared." He looked at me with bloodshot eyes still full of tears.

"I am too, but this will stop soon. I know it will." I rubbed his back.

"You keep saying that, but it hasn't happened yet." He pulled at the grass beside him and threw it into the trickling water.

"But it will. No one said this was going to be easy." I reached for his hand. He gripped it loosely with our fingers entwined.

"I know, but I didn't know it would be this hard." He sighed and stared off across the creek, gazing like he did when he daydreamed.

"I know." I paused, following his gaze across the

creek to the overgrown brush. "I didn't either."

Derek put his head on my shoulder and allowed a few more tears to flow. I wrapped my arm around him and held him tight, running my thumb over the edge of his undershirt through his blue polo. I wanted to comfort him, but I didn't know what else to do, what else to say, what else to give the man who deserved more than I had ever given him.

"It's going to be alright," I said. Derek looked up at me and nodded.

We eventually headed back toward the house once the steam had died down and the firemen were doing a walkthrough of the debris, trying to determine the cause of the fire. I let out a sigh when I saw what was left of it, nothing but a black, charred mess of ash and wood. The bottom half of the back wall was the only thing left standing, propped up by a pile of timbers once used to support the roof, and the bubbling mound of white sludge in the center - I realized - was the industrial freezer we were planning to keep our garden vegetables in.

"Gentlemen." A man in a black and yellow uniform approached us from the debris. "I'm Chief Bill with the Fire Department."

"Yes sir. Do you know what happened?" I reached for Derek's hand. Chief Bill glanced at, cleared his throat, and continued.

"Shirt stuffed in a container of gasoline. Classic jar bomb. Some kids must've done it. You had any trouble with those Rebels?"

"Yes. For about a month and a half now."

The Chief let out a long sigh and pulled a piece of paper from his pocket.

"Have they left you anything like this before?" He unfolded it and passed it to us. I gasped.

"Oh my, God," Derek covered his mouth.

"We found it wrapped around a brick in the driveway. We think it was used to break one of the windows."

Hastily scribbled on the paper was a drawing of stick figure hanging from a noose and one word: Michael.

My breath left me as if someone had stepped on my chest. I felt like someone had taken a pitchfork, shoved it down my throat, roasted me over a fire, and fed me to a pack of rabid wolves. My eyes began to swell with enough tears to put out the flames and my heart throbbed in my throat.

"This is your fault," Derek's voice was cold.

"What?" I stared at him - one tear escaped down my cheek.

"We could've avoided this weeks ago, but you said it

181

would stop. You said people would get used to it. You said we could be happy here."

"You're not happy?"

"Are you?"

"No, but-"

"Exactly! We've been miserable ever since we got here!" He raised his voice. "But you were the one who convinced and sabotaged me into moving to a place where people want to murder our son!"

"Sabotaged?" I started raising my voice.

"You wouldn't take no for an answer. You wanted to live here and that was that."

"You should've said something!"

"How could I when you're the one who thinks everyone is accepting of the gays?!" His voice echoed across the flood plain, eliciting stares from some of the firemen and neighbors who had come out to watch. I stood there in shock at his question and for the first time in our relationship, I didn't have any words.

"You know, I entered into this relationship, this commitment to you, because I love you," his voice was calmer now, "but to constantly deny a problem because you believe in the goodness of humanity, to put our whole family in danger, you've crossed a line."

"I wouldn't let anything happen to you or Michael."

"You let this happen." He swiftly gestured towards the smoldering garage.

He let everything out, everything he had been holding inside since the day he met me, how I always have to have my way, how I always had to have the last word, how I needed constant reassurance of his commitment, how everything in the house had to be spotless. I just stood there, unable to speak or refute anything, hanging on every word that spilled out into the spinning air.

"You can be such a girl sometimes; you know that? I wanted a husband, not a wife," he said. My jaw dropped at his insult. I've been called a lot of things, but that was the worst. It was my Achilles Heel and he shot it with the only arrow that could penetrate it.

"You son-of-a-bitch." I collapsed to my knees in the dead grass, tears streaming down my face in torrents, like waterfalls after a heavy rain. I sobbed harder than I ever had, choked on my own saliva, coughed and spat, couldn't breathe. My eyes were clamped as closed as an airtight door on a battleship, shutting out the chaotic world and the man who wrenched my bleeding heart in two.

How could he do this? How could the man who claims to love me hurt me so much? I wanted to run, to just get up and run as fast and hard as I could away from the world, away from the pain, away from everything. At that very moment, the world felt cold, dark. Empty. I prayed for rain to fall and drown me in my own despair and drag me to the depths where no one would ever find me again, down to where the light never reaches, down to where the Earth still keeps many secrets.

But rain didn't fall. I didn't get pulled into the depths of the ocean. Instead I felt the warmth of hands lifting me from the cold ground, carrying me through the blackness I kept myself immersed in. The darkness swirled and shifted, both finite and boundless, freeing and constricting. I heard whispers in the distance, figures gliding through the void, felt more than seen. I heard a young boy that reminded me of Michael crying, no not crying, laughing. I heard a woman say something I didn't understand in the sweetest voice, sweet like peanut butter fudge. I strained to listen, but it was gone the second I tried to focus on it.

Suddenly my stomach churned like the feeling you get on the initial drop on a roller coaster, and I landed on something cold and soft. The darkness around me gradually changed to an endless horizon of silver glass and white light. Silhouetted against the sun, a man walked toward me, his steps as fluid as water. I called out to him, asking his name, but he never replied. He came to rest just out of arms reach, his face still blacked out by the sun. A million questions ran through my mind, but before I could ask him anything, he turned to me and said, "I'm sorry. I love you."

The bright light started to dim and the man faded into the silver glass and white light, leaving me to stand alone against another onslaught of darkness. I started to scream at the void, cursing it for the misery it brought me, but an invisible hand began to shake me.

I awoke in my bed, still screaming, sitting upright, Derek holding me tightly in his arms.

"Shhh, its ok," Derek said.

I looked at him, then to the window. The sun had set and all of the firemen were gone, leaving only a driveway soaked in water from the earlier events. I looked back at Derek, perplexed as to why he was still there. Hadn't he just told me all of the reasons he hated being with me? Wouldn't he just rather be alone?

He noticed my puzzled look and took my hand in his, running his thumb slowly over mine. He told me I had passed out in the front yard, and that he realized that despite everything he said, he loved me too much to let me go. He picked me up and carried me inside to bed and Trish and Bobby brought Michael home. He was just about to go to crawl into bed when he noticed that I was twitching in my sleep, something I only do when I'm having a nightmare, so he climbed in next to me and held me close until I stopped shaking.

"Did you mean all of those things you said earlier?" I asked, still resting in Derek's arms.

"Yes, but I wouldn't have you any other way. You're stubborn, and that's why I married you."

I couldn't help but smile.

"I love you," Derek said, squeezing me a little bit more.

"I love you, too, and you know, we should call the police this time."

"Didn't have to. They were arrested for drinking underage and driving under the influence an hour after they set fire to our garage. With all of their previous offenses, they'll be put away for a while."

"Good."

I collapsed onto my pillow, exhausted, and Derek wrapped his arms around me and pulled me into his chest. I could feel our hearts beating together as we drifted off into each other's warmth.

***

A year has gone by without another incident. We've become the happy family I imagined ourselves being when we moved here. Michael is enjoying Kindergarten and he and Bobby are the best of friends. Derek rebuilt the garage and added a sunroom, and I've started a new job with Family Matters, an organization that helps troubled kids. Derek and Michael are my life and I'll always cherish the two people who make my life worth living, but I'll never forget the day it almost crashed to a halt, the day that marks my heart like an appendectomy, fully mended, invisible to others, but always visible to me.

ABOUT THE AUTHOR

Will Brooks was born and raised in Central Kentucky. He graduated in 2014 with a Bachelor of Science in Music from Murray State University. He writes in his spare time and currently lives in Las Vegas with his husband, Lee.

For more from Will Brooks, now Will Spargur, please visit:
williambrooks9455.wix.com/willspargurauthor
or follow him on Facebook at:
www.facebook.com/willspargurauthor

www.ingramcontent.com/pod-product-compliance
Lightning Source LLC
Chambersburg PA
CBHW060206070426
42447CB00035B/2764